Sea Edge

PHILLIP KELLER
© 1984

W. Phillip Keller

Sea Edge

WORD BOOKS
PUBLISHER
WACO, TEXAS

A DIVISION OF
WORD, INCORPORATED

Acknowledgments: The twenty-one chapter illustrations are by David J. Anderson. All others by the author.

SEA EDGE

Library of Congress Cataloging in Publication Data

Keller, W. Phillip (Weldon Phillip), 1920-
  Sea edge.

  1. Meditations.   I. Title.
BV4832.2.K415 1985   242   84-20961
ISBN 0-8499-0457-9

Printed in the United States of America

To
Those who love the sea edge and
sense God's presence there

Phillip Keller.
© 1984.

Contents

*"Sing unto the Lord a new song,
and His praise from the end of the earth,
ye that go down to the sea, . . ."*

Isaiah 42:10

1.

My Bit of Beach

From the first hour that I strolled, barefooted, along the shimmering sands of this remote bit of beach I fell in love with it. It lay warm, secluded and peaceful at the base of rugged cliffs that had faced the surge of a thousand Pacific storms.

It was not an easy piece of coastline to find. Vague rumors had reached me from time to time that this stirring shoreline was a favorite wintering ground for scores of seabirds. I was told that seals and sea lions came here to rest on the rocks that stood out to sea. Reports came in that it was a choice location to watch the whales in their migration; schools of porpoises at play; pelicans diving for fish; and only once in a while, a solitary person taking a quiet stroll.

It had taken patience and endurance to discover the spot. I followed every road and scrambled down any cliff trail that led toward the ocean edge. Some trails came to empty dead ends. Even more were closed to public access. Then, at last, one sunny afternoon in early May I clambered down a steep, broken bank overgrown with wild beach peas and found my bit of beach.

Gulls, dressed in their immaculate white breeding plumage, wheeled in the wind. Their wild cries, so sharp and piercing, cut through the roar of the surf below them. Across the breakers came the harsh bark of sea lions challenging each other for their favorite ledge on the rough rocks at sea.

Flocks of sanderlings, flying in tight, flashing formations swept up and down the sands, their glinting wings reflecting the warm afternoon sun like shining mirrors of silver.

A profound sense of peace swept over me. It was every bit as real and palpable and strong as the incoming tide running across the golden sand. Here was intense inspiration of spirit, as tangible as the warm thermals rising against the sun-drenched ramparts of rock soaring above the beach. Everywhere there was beauty, splendor—the eternal impact of my Father's wondrous design conveyed to me in grandeur and loveliness.

At such moments—interludes of intense delight and keen spiritual perception—our inner souls long with exquisite yearning to know that somehow they shall endure. And little did I dream on that sun-splashed spring day, seven years ago, that in God's own good time, my permanent home would be perched on a height of land just a few hundred yards from this special spot.

Such is the gracious touch of God's hand upon our little lives. It is His generous pleasure to give us dreams. It is His unique habit to help us see those fond hopes come to exciting reality and heart-pounding fulfillment. This is all part of the exquisite wonder of knowing Him as a dear companion.

That first day of my discovery I little realized that this bit of beach would become one of the most familiar spots in all the world to me. I never anticipated that I would stroll along this sea edge hundreds of times in the years ahead. I could not envision the days without number that I, and only I, in company with Christ, would spend precious hours alone upon this sun-kissed strand.

But He did!

He knew all about the quiet hours in this place.

He saw the lessons I would learn from Him along this wave-washed shore.

He, and He alone, was aware how I would be nourished by each breath of so much space and light—such sharp, cool, clean air from the vastness of the ocean.

Here He would, through the sea and sand and sun and surf, disclose to my heart eternal principles that stirred me to the depths. Here I would understand some of the mystery of His ways with man. Here He would speak to me in terms a common man, like myself, could clearly grasp with acute perception.

From this bit of sea edge He has shown me, dramatically, tremendous truths in the form of ocean parables. These cameos of His own greatness are not mine alone to be hugged only to my heart. They are a legacy for all of us who have come to know and love Him.

Here they are shared in simple, precise word pictures. May they endure long after my footprints have left this lonely, lovely shore, to tread instead upon the eternal strand of a new eternity . . . far beyond my bit of beach . . . in the presence of His Person.

"Song-o'-the-Surf"
10 December 1983
California

2.

_____

Ocean Majesty

The ocean draws me to itself with a powerful, yet gentle magnetism, calling to my soul with strains not always audible to the ear. It moves upon my spirit in magnificent majesty.

Though I have lived in close company with the ocean for many seasons, my awe has never waned—its wonder has never dimmed. Every time I step upon its shore, its broad expanse, sweeping away to the utmost horizons, captures my heart. I am caught up in the grandeur of its might—humbled, stirred and moved by its glory.

I am a man who must have space—wide expanses, long views and sweeping vistas—to thrive. These are as essential to my free spirit as is the wind to my lungs. I cannot be cramped in the narrow confines of man-made corridors fashioned from sterile concrete, cold steel or glinting glass.

Perhaps in part this is the result of my somewhat wild and untamed heritage: the wide expanses of the open sun-splashed African plains, the long vistas of distant hills dappled blue by moving cloud shadows, the great brooding mood of a realm not yet marred by man.

All of these have precise counterparts in the ocean expanse that sweeps away to the south on my bit of beach. Every time I approach the cliff top and hear the muted sounds of the sea at work on the beach below, a thrill of anticipation—eager, keen, and pulsing—surges through me. The trail winds down through a deep draw. Each step down provides an ever widening vista of the ocean spread out beneath the sky.

This path is really like a little pilgrimage.

It always ends at the same place—the sea edge.

Yet every new day is alive and fresh, and I am filled with anticipation.

It is this same vitality that is a large part of the ocean's magnetism, for it is not sterile. It is not cast in concrete. It is not fixed in place or arrested in action.

Everywhere I look there is motion, life, energy. The endless vitality of its environment engulfs me. I am surrounded with the vigor of its energy. The mighty movements of its tides, waves, sea currents and ocean breezes enfold me in their irresistible embrace.

This sea edge is a special world.

At best I can do no more than stand upon its shore and sense that I am but a minute particle of humanity on the edge of an ocean stretching around the globe. Its magnitude is beyond imagination. Its depth, its width, its length are beyond my measurement. Its power and dynamic action linked to moon, sun, stars and all the constellations of outer space are beyond my finite understanding. It is often a realm cast in dramatic light.

So I am stilled before its majesty.

My soul is silent in its presence.

There is assurance in its might.

Few, few indeed, are the mornings when I stroll along this shore that the ocean does not so impress me with its power, its glory and its majesty. I am humbled in its company. I am awed by its magnificence. Yet, wonder of wonders, I am also made glad to be with it.

For you see, strange as it may sound, though I was born and grew up hundreds of miles from the ocean, and was for years a stranger to it, I have come to love it. The ocean has drawn me to itself and won my total allegiance.

I really am an ocean lover.

In profound ways the sea has wooed my soul.

It has made me a part of its own life.

Just as much as the waves breaking on the smooth sand are an integral part of this wondrous world—or the gulls gliding along the cliff face, or the seals thrusting through the currents—so am I, as a solitary man, leaving the footprints of my small steps on the ocean edge.

All is passing. All is in motion. All is change—new every day, fresh in every way. None of it will stay. Only the ocean endures, eternal, unending in its movements.

So it is that these deep reflections and long thoughts move smoothly but surely into the realm of my spirit. In His own gracious and gentle way God has spoken to me more emphatically through parallels in the sea than any sermon in a sanctuary.

For to me, it seems, His majesty, His might, His splendor are as magnificent as any seascape. In quietness as I contemplate His character it equals and surpasses in grandeur anything known to man. The extent of His glory fills the earth.

As I am drawn to Him by the irresistible magnetism of His own greatness, there are pensive moments when in awe and wonder I sense that at best I can only really experience "the edge of His life." There is a dimension, at least in my earth life, in which He will never be known in all His magnificence. With my human fallibility and spiritual limitations I shall never fully comprehend the length or depth or breadth of His infinite, amazing love.

But, what joy, I still can touch the edge of His glory. I still am drawn into the intimacy of His presence. Coming softly to stand before His Majesty, I am moved by the touch of His life upon mine.

21

The innermost response of my spirit to His magnificent presence is, "O Lord, my Father, my Creator, my Most High God! You are here! All is well!"

Human language is strained to describe the sense of ecstasy, the upwelling of blessing, the surging tide of serenity that floods over my soul in such moments. This is an interaction between God and a common man made doubly precious because I was once a stranger to this One. I knew nothing of the inspiration of His Spirit. I was ignorant of and oblivious to the impact Christ's character could make on mine.

Just as the ocean sculpts and shapes my bit of beach with the rise and ebb of every tide, so there sweeps now across my soul the surging impulses of God's own gracious Spirit. The powerful current of the very life of Christ sweeps through my mind, my emotions, my will to do His own wondrous work.

Still I sense profoundly that I am, like my bit of beach, but a single soul on the bare edge of God's great love. But I am there—open, exposed, vulnerable, susceptible to every incoming surge of His Spirit, able to be altered, waiting to be worked upon, shaped and re-created daily by the impulse of His presence.

The beach does not shape itself!

It is a reflection of the movement of ten thousand ocean tides. It is the product of the ocean's might and power. It is the superb piece of artistic craftsmanship that emerges from the ocean's endless sculpting.

Nor am I a self-made man.

For there has played upon my life the eternal impact of the love of God in Christ which has shaped my character with eternal perseverance.

3.

High Tide

No two days are ever exactly the same on my bit of beach. Part of its great appeal lies in the ever-changing appearance of its shoreline.

The subtle play of sunlight and shadow on the cliff faces alters their contours. Some mornings the rugged rocks seem softened by the muted pastel shades of the rising sun. They glow warm, golden, wrapped in sunshine and serenity.

Other days the same rock buttresses stand gray and forbidding in the fog and mist that swirls in off the sea. The shoreline looks almost black, dark with dampness, soaked with sea spray.

Always, always, always the ocean is at work on the land. Summer and winter, spring and autumn the changing tides rise and ebb shaping the character of the coast. Their force is utterly relentless—their power immeasurable—their titanic thrust untamed.

Great mysteries surround the majestic, awesome action of the tides. With incredible precision they move billions of tons of water from surface to surface upon the sea. They are the reflection of gigantic energy within the cosmos that knows no rest, that never slumbers, that never sleeps.

Hour after hour, year in and year out, for eons of time the tides have risen and fallen, then risen and fallen again upon this shore. They are a part of the fundamental creative forces set in motion by divine design to shape and sculpt the shore. Their work is never done. Their impact is ever there. Their polishing goes on toward perfection.

Amid all this constant action at the ocean edge, one of its most compelling interludes is the time of high tide. This is the hour when the beach appears to be its smallest. Trillions of tons of sea water have come surging into the seascape to flood into every cove and tide pool. Where before there had stood stretches of sand, reefs of rock or buttresses of basalt, now there shimmers the silver mantle of the sea.

The sea is everywhere. It flows with smooth swells over the rocks, over the inlets, over the accumulated debris deposited here by a thousand storms. The sea is bright, shining, like quicksilver running into every tiny crevice or rivulet that lies upon the shore.

All the ugliness of flotsam and jetsam cast up here by stormy gales is covered by the incoming sweep of the high tide. Every deformity, every gaunt and grim bit of junk that may have been deposited on this strand by the careless hand of man is hidden from view.

In its place there pulses back and forth the stirring sight of sparkling waves that break against the banks in a flashing spray of green and white water. Everywhere the ocean is moving logs, shifting stones, rearranging the contours of the shore. It will never be quite the same as it was before high fashioned. This is when, beneath the water's impact, eternal endless changes are wrought in wondrous ways.

This thrust and change brought to my bit of beach by extreme high tides has always thrilled me. The apparent

nd corresponding contraction of
me a profound lesson in my life

nes, when in His own gracious,
mes flooding over my little life.
the "high tide" of His powerful
my soiled and shabby soul. There
anything else I must have that
sublime sense of His Spirit sweeping into every secret cove
and inlet of my life.

The world is so much with me. The careless hand of man,
the cruel ways of our society, the thoughtless acts and omitted
courtesies of my contemporaries leave a legacy of hurts and
sorrow and wreckage in my life—the black rocks of rising
anger, the hard jagged reefs of dark resentment, the flotsam
and jetsam of ill will that clutter my character.

Only Christ can change all this. Only He can alter the
contours of my disposition. Only He can displace the debris
of my soul with the surging newness of His own person.
There must be an exchange of His life for mine—of His
desires for my, otherwise, selfish impulses.

It is He, who in the high tide of His relentless patience and
perseverance, presses in upon my person.

I cannot, dare not, keep Him out. It is His eternal, sure
in-coming, as inexorable as the rising tide, that gives hope for
covering all the corruption and defilement of my days.

Those of us who wish to be utterly honest with ourselves
and with our Father know full well the need of His covering.
We cry from the depths: "Who can cover my iniquities? Who
can enfold me in righteousness? Who can fill me with the
fullness of God?"

It is He and only He who can do this for us.

There is no one else.

And we must see this.

The beach does not cover itself.
It is covered by the sea.
The shore does not change itself.
It is shaped by the tides.
The sea edge does not diminish its own size.
The ocean does this as it sweeps in upon it.

The alterations and rearrangements of the coast are the eternal work of the eternal tides.

And in my life as one who lies open, exposed and receptive to the action of The Most High, it is He who will cover and conform me to His own pattern of ultimate perfection. He does not relent. He does not rest. He neither slumbers nor sleeps. It is He who is at work upon my soul and within my spirit both to will and to do according to His own grand designs.

The incoming of Christ by His sublime Spirit always changes the contours of our lives. Once we have been filled with all the fullness of His grace and goodness we are never the same again. His presence can inundate every crevice, can fill every corner of our convoluted lives.

Yes, there are days and there are times when only the high tide of God's overflowing goodness can put right all that is wrong within. Most remarkable, those looking on will know and sense the impact of His life on mine. For I am His bit of beach!

At high tide the surging ocean asserts itself with awesome power upon the open shore. Likewise in my life, the impact of God's pervasive Spirit, if allowed to do so, can move in majestic might upon my soul and spirit and body.

As the full weight of the sea currents change and shape the coast, so Christ, in control, recreates me as a man. He alters the contours of my character and conduct.

At full flood the tide turns the entire beach into a glistening expanse of water, brilliant as a sheet of beaten silver. And thus it is my Father enfolds my common life in the generous love and purity of His own perfection.

Little wonder John cried out from the depths of his yearning spirit: *"He must increase, but I must decrease!"* (John 3:30).

4.

Breakers

Yesterday morning I stood at the edge of the cliffs and gazed up and down the coast. It was a spectacular scene of blue and white beauty. Though I have watched the winter breakers crash in thundering foam along this shore a thousand times, they still stir me to the depths.

From high vantage points atop the bluffs one can see up and down the length of the land for several miles in both directions. Here, in great bursting sheets of curling spume and white spray, the blue waters of the Pacific boil and roll against the beach.

The giant waves, spawned a thousand miles away in the uncharted depths of the ocean, have moved with enormous momentum across vast distances to come crashing on this coast. In a magnificent, surging, spilling, breaking action, ten million tons of water thunder on the sand. Approximately every six to sixteen seconds a fresh new breaker bursts into foam that rumbles and surges over the shore.

It is a sight as spectacular as any giant waterfall. For what the surf may lack in height it more than makes up for in extent. Its action is a thundering sea that spreads itself in wild display for miles along the continental ledge. Its untamed music is a song of splendor and glory, a song of the sea in motion, a song of the ocean at work upon the land.

Yet the outer grandeur of the breakers is not their only honor. For within the waves themselves there goes on a magnificent cleansing movement of the beach.

This inner action of the sea upon the shore is seldom understood by those who come here only casually. It is as if the curling foam, with countless flying fingers combs and scours the sand for any debris or silt that pollutes the shore. Caught up in the scrubbing, scouring, washing action of the rolling breakers every trace of the contamination is borne away into the sea itself.

As the waves wash across the sand and crash around the rocks, they run back in ceaseless motion carrying off the silt and mud that may have marred the shore. In wondrous ways the ocean currents carry this burden of sediment in suspension. Lifting it from the land, they finally lay it down in the remote depths of its own immensity. Thus the sea deposits the accumulated filth of the years in far-off ocean canyons.

It is a perpetual process. The poured out power of the breaking waves washes the beaches, yes, my bit of beach, with meticulous care. It is the life, the energy, the dynamic of the sea that spills out upon the shore to cleanse it from all its contamination.

Here a titanic interchange goes on endlessly. The ocean waters—clear, clean, fresh and pure—pour out upon the polluted sands. There they pick up the decaying debris, the bird feces, the fallen feathers, the flotsam and jetsam that would otherwise stain the shore. In their grasp the grime is gone, transported away into the ocean deeps. In place of the pollution there is left behind by the breakers, shining sand and polished rocks.

So the breakers restore the beach, cleansing its shoreline and leaving the sea edge bathed in pristine purity.

Reflecting quietly upon this titanic transaction between sea and land, I have been deeply moved by the profound parallels that lie between my soul and God. As I meditate upon the majestic mysteries of His dealing with me I can clearly comprehend some similarities that have helped me understand the magnificence of His person, the magnitude of His intentions toward me.

For just as the ocean is ever at work breaking itself over my bit of beach, so my Father's unfathomable love is ever in action spilling out upon my sin-stained soul. Had He chosen, as well He might, to confine His compassion to Himself, I would never have known the cleansing, caring impact of His life on mine.

Like the breakers crashing every few seconds upon the shore, so His love comes sweeping over my soul from out of the eternal depths of His own infinite being. Over and over His life is broken on my behalf.

Christians, it seems to me, speak too glibly, too lightly, too flippantly of the cleansing blood of Christ. They treat it almost as a talisman that can be called upon in a moment of extremity.

It is more, much more than that! It is instead the eternal, everlasting, endless life and love of God Himself being poured out in unrelenting power upon us poor mortals. His majestic body broken on our behalf, spilled out in ten thousand times ten thousand actions of self-giving, self-sacrifice is for our cleansing—for our salvation.

Not until we, in awe, wonder, and humility, see the grandeur of His generosity that allows His pure life to surge over our pollution will we ever repent. Only then can we begin to grasp even a little of the wondrous work the breakers of His spilled-out love can effect in our experience.

Just as the sea absorbs into itself all the debris from the shore, bearing it away into the fathomless oblivion of its own depths, so Christ bears in His own person all the wrongs and ill will of our contaminated characters. He receives into His infinite forbearance all our wretched attitudes, our contorted decisions, our negative impulses. In their place He pours out His love, His care, His forgiveness upon us—new each day—wave upon wave.

The unique disclosure given to us by His own Spirit, goes beyond even this, namely, that all of our sins and all of our iniquities are carried away into the depths of the sea of His forgiveness. Not only to be buried from view but also forgotten forever. Only God our Father could be so gracious. Only He could be so magnanimous. Only He could be so utterly astonishing.

In a word, to use the theological terminology of the New Testament, "He hath made him to be sin for us, who knew no sin; that we might be made the righteousness of God in him" (2 Corinthians 5:21). What an exchange!

There is enormous beauty in this transaction, a beauty that surpasses the breakers flinging themselves upon my bit of beach. There is also an eternal cleansing action in Christ's life laid down, spilled out upon my behalf to cleanse and purify me. That, too, transcends the eternal washing of the shore by the endless waves breaking over it.

The breakers make the beach beautiful both without and within. Likewise the outpouring of the love of God upon my life—the eternal, endless energy of His own person—purifies my character and beautifies my behavior.

The cleansing of the beach is one of the special secrets of the sea.

And the cleansing of my soul is one of the great mysteries of God's love for me—a love so great it stills my soul, it humbles my heart, it subdues my spirit.

5.

Beauty on the Beach

After every storm, after every high tide, after the powerful action of the combers that have cleansed the beach, there remains behind remarkable beauty. Not just the outward splendor of a wave-washed shore sparkling in the sun, but an intimate beauty of delicate design etched upon the sand, carved upon the cliffs.

This character of a coast line is ever changing. It never remains static. It does not become sterile and stale. Each new day makes a difference in its design. Every high tide alters its outline. Endlessly the sea edge is shaped into a myriad of fascinating seascapes.

Some days the shore, glistening like polished gold, has draped along its edge a delicate lacework of silver filigree. A thousand tiny wavelets moving on and across the sand, like a master-weaver's loom, fashion a blue and white embroidery on the beach. Its fabric flashes with the brilliant sequins of ten million bubbles that reflect the light as they burst into splinters in the surf.

The pattern of the spume that spreads itself upon the sand is of infinite, interacting fragments of white foam. It lasts but a few moments, caught briefly in intense beauty upon the eye of the onlooker. Then it is swept clean, carried away into the next incoming wave, to be replaced by another, equally arresting.

Everywhere there is action, motion, life and design. Picture upon picture is created in rapid succession on the shore. No two are identical, no two even appear similar. Each is a unique creation formed by the ebb and flow of the sea upon the sand. The shore is the master artist's canvas, the wavelets His sure, swift, brush strokes.

As the sea recedes on the falling tide it leaves behind a legacy of wondrous beauty. The tiny, hairlike rivulets of ocean water draining from the sand shape whole "forests" of little trees in the porcelainlike surface of the shore. Their design is as exquisite as any pattern hand painted upon the most precious bone china. The "tide trees" are always shown in winter garb, stripped of their leaves, bare, with bold trunks and smooth branches, drawn upon the still wet surface of the sand.

There are gorgeous undulations left upon the sea edge by the ebbing tide. The cutting, swirling, rhythmic movement of the ocean currents shape the contours of the tide flats and sand dunes into smooth, soft curves that soothe the eye and still the soul. It seems almost an indiscretion to step upon their pristine perfection.

Here and there the dainty web of a crab's tracks or a sea bird's footprints only add to the intensity of their lingering loveliness. Especially in late evening, or at early dawn, when the long low light accents their smooth forms into bas-relief, their beauty is so sharp, so stabbing, it almost pains.

Even the smoothing of stones, the polishing of rocks, the fashioning of driftwood by the oscillating action of the waves leaves one lost in wonder, awe and quiet gratitude for such gracious gifts from the sea. Everywhere one walks there is left the impress of the tides that work, often unseen, upon this bit of beach.

The high cliffs of sandstone, the rugged headlands of dark rock, the reefs and tide pools sculpted by the rasping thrust of a thousand storms are each a fine and splendid masterpiece. Each has been touched and transformed by the mighty power of the deep.

All of this beauty on the beach, all of these rare and delicate designs, all of the exquisite sea-edge forms are the fashioning of the tides. Every ocean current that swirls along the coast cuts and chisels as surely as any sculptor's tools. Every wave or wavelet washing against the land rasps and shapes with relentless artistry. Every ton of sea water pressing upon the beach compresses the shore into a special seascape.

So it is, too, with the impact of the presence and power of God Himself upon my soul.

It is the eternal persistence of His splendid Spirit that, working upon my mind, emotions and will, gently conforms them to His own wishes.

It is the compassion of Christ's love, the incoming waves of His wondrous grace that flood over me day upon day to submerge my spirit in Himself.

There, often unseen by the world, unrecognized by my contemporaries, unnoticed, even by my most intimate associates, He fashions me to the unique pattern of His special design for me. No two of us are ever exactly the same. Each is a "one-of-a-kind" creation shaped by the Master's hand.

In Christian circles it becomes increasingly common to hear the remark, "He is a beautiful person" or "She is a beautiful soul." It is really a carry-over into the church from a crass culture which exalts so-called "beautiful people"—a synonym for the sophisticated, wealthy, upper set of society.

Amongst God's people the definition of true beauty is not in terms of charm, charisma or the subtle flatteries of fashion, outward appearance or pride. It is, rather, beauty of behavior, loyalty of life, serenity of spirit.

These attributes of character and perfection of personality are seldom the sort to attract public acclaim. They are hardly the hallmark of those men and women adored by the world.

For, even of our Lord it was said, "He hath no form nor comeliness; and when we shall see him, there is no beauty that we should desire him. He is despised and rejected of men; a man of sorrows, and acquainted with grief. . . " (Isaiah 53:2, 3).

The world's estimation of "beauty," and God's evaluation of beauty in His people, are sometimes poles apart. And we must recognize that often the rugged character and sterling soul shaped under the formidable fashioning of the hand of God, beautiful to His eyes, may indeed be despised by our contemporaries.

Sometimes the most beautiful beach is the one which has endured the most severe storms. The most attractive sea edge has been exposed to the fiercest force of flood tides. The most spectacular seascapes are sculptured by the most sweeping wave action.

My very natural human reaction is to try to avoid the storms of life, to hide from the abrasive action of daily events, to retreat from the in-coming impact of God's providential presence in my affairs.

But let me not!

As I recognize my Father's kind hands at work upon my life, I shall be quietly content to expose myself to Him. It is in the sure knowledge that He knows full well the best way to make me attractive to His eyes that I shall rest beneath His strong hands. In His presence I shall find peace. No matter what storms, trials or stress are brought to bear upon my soul I shall see them as His tools for shaping my character into a winsome piece of His workmanship.

Because He is here, active, patiently at work on me, *all is well!*

6.

Healing Waters

From the dawn of human history men have been acutely aware of the healing properties of the seashore. Across the long centuries men and women, boys and girls have been sent to the sea for restoration of health, for rejuvenation of body.

To use an ancient British expression, "A few weeks by the sea will put it all right again." And so because of this amazing capacity to cure so many ills, the ocean edge has always been a favorite retreat for those who sought to restore their strength.

This has been true in my own life. At the rather early age of thirty-four I was invalided and sent back from Africa with less than six months to live. It was to the sun-drenched beaches of Vancouver Island I returned. There, as I lay on the sand, swam in the sea, strolled along the cliff edge, little by little strength, healing and vigor returned to me.

Now, well into my sixties, spared some thirty more years to serve my Master, I still refer to the seashore as "my health insurance." Few are the days that I do not spend an hour or two in solitude along the ocean edge.

The shore has an atmosphere of serenity, beauty, strength and invigoration that stimulates the whole of man. It is more, much more, than merely a balm for the body. As we shall see in subsequent chapters, it also has a profound impact upon our moral and spiritual lives. The sea can restore weary minds, strained emotions, flagging wills and aching hearts. But beyond all this, it can be that strong inspiration of God to lift our spirits, cleanse our conscience, and draw us to Himself.

Part of the reason that the sea possesses such potent healing properties is its content of a saline solution. It carries in suspension not only salt, but also a multitude of other trace minerals. Some of these rare substances are seldom found on land, yet they abound in the ocean.

The fact that the sea waters which wash over the coastline in a continuous scouring action are salty tends to sterilize and cleanse the shore. The salt actually counteracts decay of material that accumulates on the beach. It deters decomposition. It purifies and prevents undue putrefaction and pollution.

The result is that the beach is not only beautiful to behold, but it is also a lovely place to be. There is a fragrance, a pungent freshness, that permeates the air and quickens the senses. Part of this comes from the ozone off the sea.

There is a rich and abundant supply of oxygen in the breezes that blow in off the breakers. They are charged with moisture and trace elements that sweep in over the shore in potent stimulation.

The sea water itself is a marvelous healing agency. Cuts, wounds, abrasions, sores and skin blemishes are sterilized, cleansed and enabled to heal with great rapidity. Even injured joints and torn ligaments, if bathed in the sea, then exposed to the warm therapy of the sun, will mend in wondrous ways.

Just walking barefooted on the sand, letting the ocean

waves play about one's feet and legs is beneficial. The splash of sea water on the skin makes it throb and tingle with exquisite delight as the blood comes racing to the surface of the body.

Everywhere, in a hundred ways, the ocean waters heal.

Often, as I stroll along the shore, or sit quietly contemplating the grandeur of the deeps, the Spirit of God reminds me that similarly He is my great Healer. It is He who restores my soul. It is He who renews my spirit. It is He who imparts to my life the health and wholesomeness of His own character.

The unique disclosure given to us mortal men in God's Word is that at best we are corrupt. Our pride, our so-called self-righteousness, our perverseness are a pollution in the presence of the impeccable Person of Christ. There is a formidable force of decay and inner soul degeneracy within man.

Only the counteracting agency of the very life of God Himself can ever purge away our self-centeredness. Only the inner, sterilizing, sharp action of the self-sacrificing cross of Christ can eradicate my human corruption. Only the Spirit of God can enable me to see that my wrongs and wounds and selfish preoccupation can be corrected and healed by the touch of His life on mine. Only His love sweeping into my soul can sterilize it.

This healing, this wholeness, this wholesomeness, this "holiness" are all one and the same in God's estimation. They are simply synonymous in His view. If we are to know and relish His companionship, they are essential. Just as with the sea, there can be no restoration, no cleansing, no rejuvenation, no healing, no help, unless we are submerged beneath the overflowing fullness of His presence. We must lose ourselves in Him. We must allow His very attitudes, His disposition, His willingness for service, to inundate, touch and transform our lives, our hearts, our wills.

In Christian circles, this work of inner healing, this purification of our motives, this counteraction of God's generous love to our selfishness is sometimes called "the work of the cross" in the life of the believer.

It is just as dramatic as the action of the sea in sterilizing the shore to arrest putrefaction. It is the self-giving, self-sharing, self-sacrificing life of Christ that cuts diametrically across my selfish self-interests. It transcends the giant "I" in my soul, to pour itself out in service to God and man.

The cross in the life of God's person is more than a symbol of Calvary on the church steeple. It is more than an ornate crucifix on the church altar. It is more than a sentimental symbol of our Lord's awful agony.

The cross represents the judgment of divine justice upon sin and selfishness. It stands for the wide forgiveness of God's love and mercy extended to us in our pollution, declaring the depths to which Christ descended to restore, redeem and make us whole as His own people. This He achieved by laying down His life for us—pouring Himself out that we might be preserved and not perish in our own defilement.

This same purifying, redeeming, mighty work must proceed within my own life. Daily, in a discipline of total obedience to His will and wishes, my old, selfish life must be crossed out in conformity to His character. His Spirit must so submerge mine in counteracting power and purity that my soul shall be set free from selfishness exactly as the beach is cleared of its corruption.

This healing action brings an inner holiness—a knowledge of the wholeness within of a wholesome spirit and a righteous soul at peace with God and with good will to men.

This release from my selfishness can come only from the constant impact of His life on mine. It is the result of the subjugation of my soul by His Spirit. It is the counteraction of my inner corruption by the purity of His presence, the cleansing of my character by His cross.

It is the outgrowth of the deliberate surrender of my will to His wishes with glad abandon. It is that which happens when I allow the fullness of His wondrous life to sweep over me as the sea sweeps over the shore.

The daily impact of His life on mine brings vigor and vitality. It insures health and holiness to all of life. It assures well-being.

GOLDEN HILLS
COMMUNITY CHURCH

7.

Life from the Sea

Last evening, just before sunset, I went alone, at low tide, to stroll along the sea edge. It was very nearly a zero tide, for it was the winter solstice. As I walked along the broad expanse of the beach, laid bare by the ebbing waters, I was again impressed with the abundance of sea life.

Everywhere I turned and looked there was life, life, life—not just the movement of the sea itself in the steady ripple of small wavelets breaking over sand bars, hidden reefs and exposed tide pools. But there was the equally vibrant, exciting abundance of marine mammals, sea birds scavenging the shore line, fish flashing in the current, and mollusks clinging to the rocks.

Two small neighbor boys, bare legged and with tousled hair, were casting at the water's edge. As I paused to chat a moment one drew a beautiful sea bass from the foaming waves. It would provide a delectable dinner for him and his widowed mother. Even his dog was excited by the catch. In sheer animal joy he raced in circles on the sand as his young master gazed in youthful exuberance at the firm strong fish in his possession.

I strolled on, drawn by the startling black rock silhouettes that stood so stark against the silver sea. The setting sun, a burning crimson orb, began to glaze the world in a golden glow. It was as if amid the changing hues of sea and sky and shore, life, subtle and yet eternal, throbbed all around me.

A group of seals and sea lions, their smooth coats shining in the setting sun, moved about on the exposed rocks. Some swam smoothly in the current. A few fought for space on the rugged outcroppings of rock where they could stretch themselves with ease.

A flight of cormorants flew in from the far reaches of the channel. A score settled on the sharp pinnacle of a reef. Their jet black plumage and stiff erect stance made them appear as so many sedate clerics standing in stern consultation. Another flight came in to alight on the cliffs where they stretched their wings to catch the last warm rays of the winter sun.

Just off-shore pelicans and white-winged terns soared and dived beyond the breakers. They were taking small fish that surged to the surface of the sea in shining schools.

On the beach and in the tide pools there were innumerable tracks of crabs and sea worms, their coming and going marked by a fine-drawn series of minute indentations in the sand.

Every tide that rises here brings life in abundance. Microscopic plankton, one of the planet's greatest protein sources, abound in these rich waters. Sea weeds and ocean plant life of a hundred kinds flourish along this coast. They are all an intimate part of the wondrous web of life that thrive in the biota along my bit of beach.

Each is a gift from the sea. Each is a daily bestowal from the ocean deeps. Each is provided in innumerable abundance for all who will accept it.

As the afterglow dimmed gently along the shore I turned my steps toward home. I inhaled deeply of the pungent ozone on the evening breeze. With one long, last lingering view I watched the well-fed gulls preen themselves upon the sand. All was well and we were at peace.

In that brief evening interlude life—new life, fresh life— had come to me as well from the bounty of the sea. A new surge of well-being coursed through my bloodstream. A rich stimulus of inspiration swept into my soul. A profound sense of the presence of The Most High engulfed my spirit in quietude and serenity.

These are the abundant gifts of God our Father to us His earth children.

They come to us constantly . . . as continuously as the change of every tide, the shifting of every sea current. But they become ours only if we are there to absorb them into our little lives.

The bounties, mercies and benefits of the Lord are new every day. They are swept along the shores of our daily experience to replenish and renew our strength as God's people. The point is I must be there to partake of the life presented for my perpetuation.

The process is a dynamic, daily interaction of any living organism with its environment. Life proceeds and is preserved only so long as there is continuous correspondence between the individual body and the biota surrounding it. The day the creature ceases to draw and derive its life from its surroundings, it dies.

So it is whether it be a scallop, a fish, a sea bird or a seal. Each has life only by virtue of the fact it is feeding on the abundance supplied by the ocean around it.

Precisely the same principle applies to me—and others who claim to possess the life of God. He surrounds me on every side with the overwhelming abundance of His life. It is He who is the very environment in which I move and live and have my being. If I am to know His life, if I am to experience the energy of His presence, if I am to drink of the dynamic of

His Spirit then it is imperative that daily I must draw upon His divine provisions.

Eternal life—everlasting life, endless life—is not some single, sterile, gilt-wrapped package dropped down into my soul at a single point in time. This is a false and dreadful concept held by uncounted hosts of ill-informed Christians. Little wonder their experience of Christ is so sterile, so fossilized, so dead.

Life is a dynamic, daily interaction between an organism and its environment. As the organism enters directly into its life-giving surroundings, the energy of the biota, in turn, enters into it. Only then is there perpetuation of life.

This explains why our Lord, Jesus Christ, continually emphasized that for man to have life from above it was imperative to "eat of Him" and "drink of Him," daily! To "eat of Christ" is to come to Him every day in a deliberate act of faith, exercising our wills to expose and open our lives fully to the impulses of His Word and His Spirit. It is the entrance of His Word that gives us His life. For the words which He speaks to us, they become spirit and they become life to us as they are ingested and accepted.

"To drink of Christ" is to believe in Him implicitly. It is to assimilate His truth, His life, His spirit, His person by a deliberate function of quiet faith. We then proceed to comply with His commands, carry out His wishes, and cooperate with His intentions for us.

The net result is to find His very life surging in us and through us. We are in Christ. He is in us. We are energized by His Word, enlivened by His Spirit, and so made abundantly productive through our Father's bountiful grace.

The sea surrounds and engulfs every living form of life that is to be found along its coastline. The ocean brings life, energy, stimulation and vitality to every crustacean, every marine organism, every fish, every sea bird, every marine mammal. But each in turn, to survive and thrive in this watery world, must derive its life from the sea.

It is not enough to be surrounded by the great ocean waters. There is more to life in the sea than merely being swept to and fro in its changing tides. Each life form must be open, receptive, fully exposed to accept and absorb life and energy from the currents of the cosmos. Otherwise it becomes a shell or skeleton cast up on the shore.

So it is with the child of God.

Daily, hourly, momentarily Christ comes to us surrounding us with His Spirit. He brings to us in immeasurable abundance the resources needed for our eternal living. Yet there remains my responsibility to open myself to Him; to allow His Word ready entry to my mind, emotions and will; to permit His Spirit to invade my spirit, penetrating and vitalizing my intuition, conscience and communion with Him.

Only in this way—in stillness and quietude, in obedience and faith, in loving allegiance—can I ever know what it is to have His life, and have it more abundantly . . . now and forever.

Let my soul beware that, like some empty shell or sun-bleached skeleton, it be not cast away upon the sands of time—dead to Him, who comes to give me life.

Always, ever, I must be open, available totally to His incoming. Thus I thrive and flourish with His life.

8.

Building Breakwaters

Roughly twelve miles away from my bit of beach, along the sun-washed coast, there lies a beautiful coastal town. It is nestled between the rugged ranges of the nearby mountains and the warm sand beaches of the Pacific.

Years ago it was decided a massive breakwater should be built out into the ocean. It was agreed by engineers and architects that such a structure could shelter small craft from the storms, providing safe haven for fishing boats and pleasure vessels.

What the planners appeared to overlook were the strong coastal currents of the sea that move relentlessly along this coast. These carry enormous loads of sand and silt in suspension as they course up and down the shore, season after season.

The result has been that despite enormous sums of money expended to build this impressive structure, the sea inexorably builds up a huge sand bar at the harbor mouth. So enormous are the loads of ocean-borne sand that by the end of the winter season the entrance to this haven is virtually sealed off. The result is that ships sheltering there are literally trapped, unable to set out to sea.

But building the breakwater has produced even more formidable problems. Cut off from the cleansing, sweeping action of the tides, the harbor becomes choked with silt, slime and dreadful sludge that settles upon the floor of this haven. On the surface it appears to be a serene and placid spot with the boats reflected in the mirror of the still waters.

Beneath that tranquil scene is a veritable cesspool of pollution and corruption.

Consequently every spring, at enormous cost and labor, huge, sea-going dredges are brought in to try to clear the harbor. The massive, noisy equipment is connected to huge lengths of rusting steel pipes that carry the black sludge down the coast and out to sea.

Week after week the giant diesel-driven pumps roar and thunder trying to draw the accumulated muck, mud, sand and sludge from the harbor. It spews out from the sewage pipes in a gushing stream of ink-black filth that contaminates the beaches and stains the lovely sea.

A dreadful stench of death and decay pervades the air. The ocean is so contaminated that for weeks no one can swim in its lovely waters. And even the beach itself is scarcely fit to set foot upon until with time it has again been cleansed and washed with the incoming tides.

But beyond all of this, the building of the breakwater has so altered the natural action and flow of the ocean currents that it affects other communities further along the coast. They are deprived of the sand which otherwise would wash up to rebuild their beautiful beaches. So, in places, after a severe "blow," the shoreline stands bare and gaunt, stripped down to boulders and rocks.

Not only does this endanger the property and homes of

those who live along the shore, but it also puts them to great expense to try to save the beach. Massive truckloads of boulders, rock and stone are hauled in to try to shore up the banks. All sorts of elaborate sea walls are erected to try to provide protection from the ocean.

Yet the sea will not be held back. Year after year it presses in upon the coast, its coming as persistent as the tides.

Several years ago I used to live a short distance from the harbor. It was about a mile away, as the pelicans fly in a direct line along the water's edge. The annual ritual of dredging the harbor was regarded with disgust and revulsion by local residents. The pollution was appalling—the stench overpowering. The desecration of the beaches was disgusting.

Yet no lasting remedy has ever been found for the evils of the breakwater. No permanent solution has been devised for overcoming the defilement of the harbor. Nor is there any— for, in simple fact, man has shut out the sea! He has closed off the cleansing action of the ocean currents. He has excluded the healing, life-giving touch of the changing tides.

Often the powerful parallel so apparent in the hopeless quandary of the harbor has come home to my own spirit with tremendous force. For we human beings build our "breakwaters" against God. We erect our barriers to keep out the strong currents of Christ's life that come flowing toward us. We devise elaborate schemes and structures to hold back the impact of His Holy Spirit upon our souls.

The tragic, terrible truth is that most men and women do not want their lives left open, exposed, vulnerable to the impact of God's life upon them. They much prefer to build their snug little harbors of selfish self-interest where, they imagine, they are safe and secure in the storms of life.

The double tragedy is that what on the surface may appear to be so serene, below the surface is dark with defilement. What at first glance looks so desirable and successful, on closer examination proves to be rotten and corrupt with unspeakable pollution and insoluble problems.

During the years in which I served as a lay pastor it startled me to see how many people, even within the church, went to such great lengths to keep God out of their lives. They had built formidable breakwaters around themselves lest He come flooding into their experience.

In ignorance they had erected barriers of unbelief against Him. In fear they had fashioned bulwarks of anxiety and apprehension against Christ. In hostility and defiance they built barricades of belligerence against His Spirit.

Often these breakwaters against the incoming tides of God's grace, mercy and compassion were erected against the church, against other Christians, against God's Good News, or against the convicting action of God's Spirit. The general attitude was: "Keep out of my life."

Somehow, strange to say, many people do not seem to mind encircling a bit of the sea of God's grace in such a way that it provides them with a so-called "safe haven." They rather enjoy having a snug little sense of security within the shelter of some formal, rigid religiosity. Even the idea of the encircling wall of a creed is enough to cut off the full impact of the incoming life of Christ. The social functions of church fellowship are a sufficient barrier to preclude the powerful presence of God's Spirit flooding the soul with character changing force.

So on the surface such lives often appear respectable, proper and secure. Yet within, there lies the awful silt of sin, the sediment of selfishness, the sludge of a corrupt character.

There are as many ways to build breakwaters against God as human ingenuity can devise. There are scores of excuses that can be brought up to keep out Christ, to resist His Spirit.

The ultimate decision is mine as to what will be done with my bit of beach.

My life can be a bright, open expanse of beauty, joy and vigor for the honor of God. Or it can degenerate into a self-centered, constricted little character that is dead and corrupt with its own selfish preoccupation.

The former will be a joy to Christ and a blessing to every life that touches it. The latter will be a grief to God's gracious Spirit, a bane to those who seek shelter behind such artificial barriers.

9.

Sea Walls and Sand Castles

Though my bit of beach is still rather remote and somewhat sheltered from the pressure of people, here and there I encounter the remnants of human activity. Like almost all beaches around the world, it bears its burden of industrial and commercial debris. These are much less conspicuous here than on many coasts. Some visitors have even remarked that it remains one of the loveliest shores they have ever seen.

Yet, at the foot of the sea cliffs, where the path to the beach descends to the sands, there are shattered, broken fragments of sea walls and concrete buttresses. These were elaborate engineering attempts, made in former times, to try to restrict the relentless action of the tides and storms that crashed against the bluffs.

Lying prostrate, pathetic, half buried in the sand are sea-worn walls of brick and concrete blocks. Toppled and torn from their original sites, they lie all askew, washed over by the waves, looking like so many fallen gods. In actual fact, they are just that, for it was in the hapless protection of these pathetic structures that previous home owners had placed implicit trust.

69

But the battering of a thousand storms, the pounding of ten thousand tides, the eternal erosion of the ocean currents have all combined to reduce them to rubble. Now the cement, reinforcing steel, bricks, wire, tangled pipes and broken mortar stand in wild disarray as silent reminders of how absurd it is to try to keep the sea at bay. Even the most ingenious sea walls eventually crash down to collapse in broken wreckage.

All is for nought. All is but passing. All is change!

The very first home we were shown for sale on this coast was threatened by the collapsing cliffs on which it was built. We loved the location but dared not risk living there. Two years ago the owner spent some $50,000.00 trying to barricade the bluffs with an enormous wall of gigantic concrete bags. Still the tides surge over and around the wall. The cliffs collapse beneath the pounding shock of the surf.

Today the lovely house stands in awful peril, only a few feet from the edge of the precipice. In time, it is bound to collapse and crash to the beach below.

What happens in such horrendous terms to oceanfront homes also occurs with regular frequency to the charming sand castles built by children on summer holidays—not that many youngsters come to this beach. But the few who do, love to erect their ornate castles behind their high sea walls and deeply dug moats.

As I stroll along the sands I occasionally come across these crumbling works of happy childhood dreams. The surge of the waves, the tumbling of the surf, and in a few swift strokes all the labor is swept away into oblivion. At best there are left behind only a few seashells used to adorn the castle or a collection of smooth stones put in place to protect the walls.

Pausing to watch the action of the waves, washing either over the wreckage of sea walls or the crumbling ruins of a small sand castle, a profound sense of pathos sweeps over me. I cannot seem to ignore them. It is impossible for me to pass them lightly.

They speak to me in terms so clear and emphatic, my

attention is always arrested. For here, before my gaze, in sharp, stabbing severity stand parables of spiritual truth.

You simply cannot stop the sea. It is relentless. It is irresistible!

For me, as a man now moving gently through the lovely twilight years of life, the remnants of sea walls and sand castles always bring up poignant memories. The gracious Spirit of Christ always uses them to remind me of my own perilous past. At the same time, however, He also quietly reminds me how in spite of my own dream castles, my own strong will, so stubborn in resisting Him, He has preserved my life to this point in time.

All of us build our sand castles on the sands of time. All of us dream our little dreams of what we shall do with our lives. We dig our deep moats around those very private ambitions. We carefully erect our walls of self-protection to surround our elaborate aspirations. We shape and mold our decisions and personal choices into castles of self-interest and self-gratification.

Most of us do this happily, blithely in our youth. We behave as though there were only time, lots of time, and us. There seem to be so many years ahead, so many seasons to carry out our schemes, so many days to do our thing. We forget so soon that God is even there; and though He is, He seems as remote as the moon that turns the beach to silver at night.

Yes, not only do we plan and build and scheme and work to erect our sand castles, we also forget that the tides of time and the power of God's presence are as inexorable as the ocean tides rising in response to the gravitational pull of the moon.

For in the full flood of high tide—under the rising surge of the incoming surf, beneath the sweeping course of the ocean currents the castle—the walls, the moats, the work of our dreams—will disappear . . . lost in oblivion.

Such is the end of those aims and ambitions built in thoughtless, careless abandon without reckoning on the power of God. Beautiful but for a day, they are swept away into nothing.

And so there comes to my spirit again and again the ancient, eternal question. "Where and on what are you building your hopes?"

Is it on sand, or is it on the rock of God Himself?

What happens to sand castles takes longer with stout sea walls. Yet the same basic principles are at work.

For years and years I was building a strong sea wall of self-defense against God. It was not shaped from concrete and reinforcing steel. Instead it was fashioned from the formidable, tough, unyielding rigidity of my own self-will. It was so stubborn and determined it withstood the stresses and strains of countless storms.

I was very sure my strong will was as secure as any sea wall. It would keep the incoming tides of my Father's pervasive presence from invading my privacy. It would restrain the waves of His love and concern from washing into my life. It would exclude the impact of His Spirit upon the inner sanctum of my spirit.

For some of us it takes years for the eternal tides of Christ's coming, and coming, and coming again, to finally break down the last tough barrier of our resistance. It takes the eternal perseverance of our Father to demolish the hardness of our hearts. It takes the sweeping waves of His Spirit to finally surge over the strong bulwarks of our souls.

Then and only then, lying broken before Him—contrite in spirit, shattered in soul, repentant in genuine remorse—do we see clearly how we built our lives oblivious to His power, patience and perseverance.

Often, all there remains of our best laid schemes is wreckage.

All of it is a grim reminder: "Let your life, your character, your career be built always in the intense awareness, *'O God, You are here, I cannot keep You out.'*"

Ultimately, always, He will have the last word!

10.

Updrafts

Almost every morning that I stroll down to the shoreline I am impressed by the warm updrafts of ocean air rising against the cliffs. It is a phenomenon peculiar to this stretch of coast.

Because these beaches, unlike most of the west coast, face south they are warmed by the sun all day. Even in winter the layer of marine air lying just over my bit of beach is trapped against the high bluffs soaring above the sands and rocks at their base.

The result is to produce an unusual hothouse effect. Here temperatures are several degrees higher than anywhere else. The proximity of the open Pacific with its moderate temperatures, combined with the reflected heat from the sun-kissed cliff faces, warms the air to produce an environment of pleasant softness.

Here the sea breezes move gently above the surface of the ocean. They caress the coast as they eddy over the sun-warmed sands. Then in steady, even updrafts they rise against the bluffs with the constant pressure of their thermal currents.

So constant are these updrafts that daring young men and women who enjoy hang-gliding can ride the updrafts for hours and hours at a time. They soar above the ocean breakers as if suspended in space.

More impressive even than the human fliers are the birds that ride the thermals. Sea gulls, pelicans, hawks and lesser shore birds soar on the ocean updrafts with remarkable beauty and grace of flight. Their movements on wing are as graceful in motion as any ballerina floating across the stage of a theater.

The soaring of the sea birds has always impressed me. Not only is the essential beauty of their bodies and wings stretched out against the blue sky impressive, but so also is the remarkable ease with which they sail upward in silence and grace.

There is, beyond their beauty, a sense of pure power that presses upon them, bearing them higher and higher. There is an incredible exhilaration in their mounting up against the backdrop of clouds and open sky. There is a glad, free, uninhibited joy in their flight patterns.

They are a glorious expression of airborne artistry. The intricate circles and lines they cut against the sky are every bit as arresting as the most detailed and perfect figures carved by a classical figure skater on a sheet of ice. In every action there is precision, energy and superb performance.

Yet, the invisible, incredible secret to it all is the rising thermals lifting, suspending, moving them in the air.

One thing I have always noticed is that none of the birds ever attempt to soar when there is a downpour of rain, cold downdrafts of air in inversion, or gusty gales battering the bluffs.

At such times, with complete acquiescence to the change in climate, they simply settle quietly on the beach. There standing sedately on the sands or perched safely on some cliff-top tree, the birds gently preen themselves. They fluff their feathers into perfect position. Then they rest their wing muscles. Some even sleep briefly in utter contentment.

They are not exercised or excited because they cannot soar against the stormy skies. Knowing the sun will shine again, they simply rest quietly. They wait patiently for the rising updrafts that will bear them aloft once more.

Across the long years of my life, God's Spirit has taught me some unforgettable truths from watching birds in flight. During quiet walks along the sea edge Christ has brought home to my innermost spirit powerful parallels learned from the ocean updrafts. My Father has used the splendor of soaring birds to show me something of His own wondrous faithfulness.

For the birds along the beach, and for me as a man, life has all sorts of weather. Just because I am a child of God, does not exempt me from the downdrafts of disaster, the cross currents of calamity, or the dark, rainy, dreary days of distress. These are as much a part of the warp and woof of life's tapestry as are the sun-filled days, brisk with warm sea breezes.

The climate may be fair or foul. The winds of change may be offshore or onshore. The days may be bright or bleak.

But the ocean is always there. Its presence and its power are ever at work, seen or unseen. And ultimately its influence is beneficial and beautiful.

The birds know this. But most of us human beings forget the faithfulness of our Father. Quietly, calmly, the birds adjust their behavior to the changing pattern of their surroundings. We humans, however, fight and buck the setbacks of our surroundings. We fret and worry over the fortunes and misfortunes of our little lives. We insist on trying to soar and sail away into the heights when we should just sit still and wait upon the wind of God's Spirit to lift and guide us.

Most of us modern Christians know precious little about waiting patiently for the Lord. We prefer to use our own high-powered technology to be on an "eternal high."

Our preachers, teachers and effervescent evangelists would lead us to believe that we can always live high in the sky, soaring against the sun. Not so. This is not God's design. Nor does He arrange our affairs that way.

We are bound to have our days of rain, our times of tears, our hours of disappointment. There are bound to be blustery storms of testing, counter air-currents of frustration and nights of darkness.

But through them all, in them all, our Father is always there. He does not desert us. He does not abandon us. He is at work in the environment of our lives, persistent in pressing in upon us in ways we do not always see, much less understand.

In these difficult, grievous, heavy times He expects that we shall simply settle down quietly upon the shore of His great grace and wait patiently for Him. He does not call us to beat our way with flashing wings and spent bodies against the storms of life. He does not ask us to fight the adverse winds in fury.

He simply tells us that those who wait upon the Lord, who wait for the weather to change, who wait for Him to alter the environment, will mount up with wings refreshed. They shall fly and not grow weary, borne aloft on the fresh updrafts of His faithfulness.

For, our Father is true to His children. Just as the sun will shine again after the storms have swept my beach, so the rising power of Christ's presence will again warm the shore of my soul. The uplifting wind of His Spirit will once more bear up my spirit. Again I shall soar in strength and beauty.

There are days to rest quietly, waiting gently on the sand. There are days to rise up and ride the surging updrafts of His presence that carry me aloft into the clouds of His joyous delight and exhilaration.

11.

Solitude by the Sea

We live in a noisy, crowded, busy world. At least most people do. Jammed and crushed into the "pressure-cooker" crucibles of our contemporary cities and towns, millions of human beings know little about solitude and stillness.

The thunder of traffic twenty-four hours a day, the rumble and roar of aircraft overhead, the cacophony of loud music, blatant advertising and high-powered programs in the media invade the sanctuary of our homes.

Relentlessly the presence and pressures of other people make their impact upon us. Our bodies grow weary from the constant assault of noise, commotion and tension. Heart attacks, insomnia, ulcers and irritability are part of the price paid for such physical abuse.

Often men and women suffer enormous anxieties and stress in mind and emotions because of the constant tensions of our twentieth-century society. Without realizing it their nervous systems and mental stability are strained to the breaking point. Some eventually do succumb. Mental institutions, psychiatric hospitals and offices that claim to cure the condition are crowded with pathetic patients.

81

In the realm of man's spirit the devastation wrought by our much vaunted modern way of life is beyond measure. People are so driven and mesmerized by materialism they become slaves to insatiable desires. A thousand false voices call to them to find fulfillment in the transient, tempting pursuits of time. They are assailed by perverted propaganda which would have them believe leisure, pleasure and treasure of an affluent society will satisfy their spirits. But they do not!

Man was made for a greater good than all of these. He was made for God. And he will never find rest of soul, serenity of spirit, until he finds that repose in stillness and quietness in company with Christ.

It is for this reason, more than any other mentioned in this book, that my hours on my bit of beach are so treasured. There in the solitude afforded to me at the sea edge I constantly discover a dimension of divine serenity that is a balm to my spirit, a deep therapy to my soul.

Because of the terrain along the coast, the hills and mountains run down to the ocean. There the tides have carved out high cliffs. At the base of these bold, light-colored bluffs lie the beaches. Strolling along the shore one is shut away from all the noise and clamor of civilization and commerce on the benches of land above the beach.

Only occasionally is there even a house in view. Here and there perhaps the roof top of a cottage perched at the cliff edge can be seen. There are no roads, no cars, no noisy vehicles—simply the ocean, the sound of the surf, the cries of the sea birds and occasionally, on blustery days, the wind gusting across the cliffs.

Here there is remarkable solitude. There is a sense of stillness greater and more majestic than mere silence. It is the hush and quietness of a small fragment of the planet still in its pristine state. It is the solace of a bit of beach not yet polluted or ravaged by the grasping hand of man.

Strolling on this ocean strand I sense that I am alone, yet

not alone, one solitary man moving quietly, gently in awe before The Most High. It is not that I have earned or deserve the privilege of such precious privacy. But rather it is the fundamental fact that I discipline myself to take the time to seek the stillness of this shore. It is there for others to share. Yet few will ever deliberately seek solitude.

Many are afraid to be alone with their thoughts. They are intimidated by the idea of spending several hours in stillness, allowing God's Spirit time to speak to them.

I have been ridiculed, both privately and in public, by those detractors who insist that the measurement of a man's usefulness is how busy he is. It is the unwritten rule of our contemporary society, both within the church and outside it, that our effectiveness is directly proportional to how much we are on the go—for God, or man.

The truth is, our Father calls us, at times, to come apart and be still before Him. Christ calls us to commune with Him in meditation and quiet contemplation of His character. The Holy Spirit calls us to serenity and rest so that we may be sensitive to His wishes.

Of course it can be argued that different people can find their privacy and seclusion in different places. There are all kinds of so-called "prayer closets." It is inevitable that there must be. The important point is, that each of us who claim to be God's children need quietude alone with Him.

For me, the ultimate in solitude is often found on the wave-washed shore, several hundred yards from my front door. There I go with a towel in hand to spread on the sand or rocks; a small well-worn Bible; or a good book; and a spirit of eager anticipation ready to listen, eager to respond to the impulses of Christ's Spirit.

Nor does He disappoint me.

For it is there we meet in quiet communion, one with another.

Being alone on the beach has some remarkable advantages

83

not apparent to the stranger. There are no interruptions in these precious interludes—no telephones, no doorbells, no mail delivery, no one calling for attention, no neighbor's dogs, or police sirens, or roaring motorcycles, or raucous radio noises.

Peace pervades the shore.

The song of the surf fills the air.

A sublime, intense sense of God's presence is everywhere.

In this arresting atmosphere I feel wonderfully free—open before my Father, relaxed in communion with Christ, uplifted by His wondrous Spirit.

As He speaks to my spirit, there is often an audible response on my part. In such a setting I can give thanks aloud. If so impelled I can hum a hymn or sing a song of joyous praise and exultation in the greatness of my God.

The gulls don't mind my melodies. Sometimes a seal will raise his head above the surf to see whence the sounds come. Occasionally the ground squirrels scrambling along the cliff face will stop to whistle in the wind at my singing.

But we are all sharing this sea edge as friends together. Great and small our Father formed us all. This is a fragment of the firmament that we revel in and rejoice over with endless gratitude.

Not all the hours at the sea edge pass in glad praise.

There are times of tears. There are sessions of intense intercession when a solitary soul pleads with His God for a world gone awry. There are acute moments of pain when deep remorse and genuine repentance are wrung out from a broken heart and contrite spirit that has grieved Christ's Spirit.

Yet for me, such encounters are more profound, more purifying, more redemptive than any service in a sanctuary.

The whole earth and sea and sky are pervaded with the presence of The Most High. Everywhere I turn there is impressed upon my still spirit the power of His majesty. Awed, amazed, stirred to the utmost depths, I stand silent, alone, serene.

A man has met his God.

A soul has been refreshed.

All is well, for God is here. Emmanuel!

12.

Sea Wind

The sea wind has a special tang to it unlike any other wind found anywhere else in the world. There is a unique, stimulating pungency to ocean breezes that stirs the senses profoundly.

There are few people indeed who do not respond with an element of excitement to the invigoration of the fresh air that moves strongly at the sea edge. It stirs the blood, refreshes the lungs, and sharpens the senses.

The sea winds along our Pacific coast, except for an occasional winter storm, come with beautiful regularity. As the southern sun warms the adjoining land during the day, ocean breezes begin to build up, blowing in over the shore from the open sea. This constant, steady flow of marine air tempers the heat of the land. It bestows a balmy, equitable climate in which plant life flourishes and human beings take great delight.

The breezes bend the fronds of the palms, rustling the slender segments of their graceful leaves like so many muted Spanish castanets. The lap of the waves, the song of the surf, the cries of the sea birds are caught up and carried ashore on the wings of the sea wind.

More than all of this, however, is the soothing, cool, therapeutic touch of the wind on one's face and arms, back, legs and entire body when bared to it. It is as if the moving air enfolds me in its embrace and holds me gently in its arms.

The ocean air caresses the cheek, massages muscles, and leaves the surface of the skin tingling with a special sensation of exhilaration and general well-being.

Because my bit of beach lies open, fully exposed to the great expanses of the South Pacific, the prevailing winds that blow across it come from afar. Some of them were spawned far out to sea. They come ashore with utter freshness, total cleanliness. They have never been contaminated with industrial pollution.

The air moving around me in my morning walks is sharp, clear and wondrously wholesome. It is charged with ozone from the ocean, brisk and clean with the pungency of the sea itself.

To inhale deeply is to sense the surge of pure drafts of air entering my lungs. The high level of oxygen in the sea wind provides a powerful impulse to my whole body. My lungs pick up the oxygen rapidly to transmit it to my blood stream. It courses through my whole circulatory system, cleansing the liver, quickening the body metabolism, stimulating the brain.

To breathe deeply of the ocean breezes is to be tremendously invigorated. It is to be fully alive, to sense the strength and vitality of the ocean itself entering my whole being.

There is something very arresting about these air movements which is reassuring. They come fresh every day. They are inexhaustible. Though not visible, they are enormously apparent. They exert a constant impact on anyone or anything exposed to them . . . they do not diminish!

Most important, not only does the sea wind surround me on every side, it actually fills my whole being within as I open myself to receive its rejuvenation. It runs its fingers through my hair; it kisses my cheek with its touch; it caresses me in tenderness; it stirs me with energy and vitality as it surges into my body.

It makes me strong and fit, alive and energetic.

Little wonder that I love to walk in the wind.

Little marvel that I relish its touch on my senses.

Little surprise that I open myself to breathe it deeply.

All of which is a vigorous response to the wind's gentle, yet persistent impress on my life. I come to love it. I relish its vitality. I revel in its invisible presence.

It is exactly the same with the wind of the gracious Spirit of God. He is everywhere present around me, though unseen to my physical eyes. His power and energy pervade the earth. His benefits enfold me on every side. His mercy and compassion come to me fresh and new every day. And if allowed to, He will enter my life, there to do His own dramatic work as surely as the sea breezes that blow along my beach.

The Word of the Lord is very specific, very precise, very clear about our life in His Spirit. He urges us again and again to walk in the Spirit. He emphasizes the need for us to be in the Spirit. He points out that we must open ourselves to His incoming. He must have entrance into our daily experience. He is the inspiration for our spirits, the stimulation for our souls, the quickening for our bodies. We are to be invaded and filled with His presence.

There is nothing magical or mystical about this. The sad tragedy is that too many Christians have made it such. They have cast a cloud of confusion over the otherwise lovely and beautiful work of God's Spirit in the midst of His people.

He comes to us constantly from out of the very depths of the greatness of God. He is ever present with us, surrounding us on every side with the wonder of His own Person. Though invisible as the sea winds He exerts His own enormous power upon the earth. He is constantly available to us. But to enjoy the dynamic of His vitality it is essential to open ourselves fully to His influence.

This takes time. It takes time to be made wholesome. It takes time to expose ourselves to the incoming of God's Spirit. It takes time to become holy as He is, the Holy Spirit of the Most High. It takes time to be still before Him and to be sensitive to His impulses and wishes.

Just as the wind off the sea is here, moving, flowing, blowing about the beach, so the wind of God's Spirit is very much at work in the world, moving mightily around us on every side.

The essential question for the Christian is, am I aware of His presence? Do I really appreciate the fact that His energy, His power, His vitality, His influence, His benefits are freely available to me?

Most of us know very little about walking in the Spirit. We are seldom energized by the reality of His presence at work upon us. We are so bundled up in the impedimenta of our human trappings that He is seldom given a chance to touch us at all. We are so insulated from His impact upon us by our preoccupation with our personal priorities, we know nothing of the stimulus that comes when we stand stripped and exposed before Him.

It takes a certain element of self-discipline to get out of a cozy home and take a tramp in the wind. It calls for courage to throw off the coat and open the shirt to let the cool breeze play upon the chest. It demands some discipline to inhale deeply of the sharp wind off the sea, to sense its vitality race through the veins and quicken the pulse. But it is worth it all to be fully alive.

So it is with the Spirit of God. He comes constantly to renew and refresh. He comes to encourage and invigorate. He comes to impart to us the resources of the Resurrected One.

It is in Him that we can find energy, power, vitality, the very dynamic for positive living . . . today.

The wind and ocean air which I inhaled yesterday will not do for today. The breezes which refreshed me last week will not so refresh me this morning. The surge of oxygen that cleansed and energized my body metabolism about a month ago will not suffice for my work this afternoon.

I must be refreshed, rejuvenated, requickened, yes, refilled each day. There is no other way. The supply and source is inexhaustible. The movement and flow is eternal. The dynamic energy never diminishes.

All that is required is that I expose and open myself before Him to be totally available to His personal impact upon me today. To so live—sensitive to His presence, aware of His wishes, obedient and open to His will—is to be filled and stimulated by His Spirit . . . now and on into eternity.

13.

Place of Peace

My bit of sea edge is a special place of peace. This strip of shoreline, that runs like a slender ribbon of sand and rock between the ocean and the land bluffs, is a small world of precious tranquillity.

On this beach of shining sand and golden rocks there rests an atmosphere of quiet repose and gentle contentment shaped by the sea. It is akin to the seclusion found in the upthrust alpine meadows of a great mountain range untrammeled by man.

My place of peace, though so close to the clamor of civilization, still remains uniquely apart from it. The high ramparts of the ocean cliffs stand guard against the commotion and conflict of the discordant sounds of human industry. The thunder of traffic, the wail of sirens, the roar of trains and planes, the bustle of business scarcely intrude here at all.

If they do, even briefly, their noise is muted by the sound of the surf, the cries of the sea birds, the song of the sea winds. Caught up in the offshore breezes, the intruding disturbances are carried away quickly into the immensity of the ocean. Peace returns and quietude prevails.

It is the atmosphere of repose that draws me here again and again. Enfolded in the endless, eternal action of wind, waves, tides and currents, the beach breathes serenity and strength. It is a quality of life ever harder to find in our crowded world.

This sea edge is a unique spot of seclusion and privacy. It is a place where a person can go to sit lost in thought, or take long walks thinking eternal thoughts, or repose in the sanctum of quiet communion with his Creator.

One does not have to be a saint, recluse or mystic to partake of this environment. For it casts its special spell upon the most common of us common people. From barelegged boys sitting on the wave-battered black rocks, staring out to sea, dreaming dreams, to elderly gentlemen strolling softly in the sunset of their days, there emanates the contentment found in the quiet company of the ocean.

This tranquillity settles down into the soul and spirit as softly as a sea bird settles down upon the shore. There the gulls and terns and curlews and pelicans rest on the sand, preening their immaculate plumage in peace. The beauty of their bodies, reflected in the mirror surface of the wet and shining shore, is etched in soft shades of gray, brown and ivory white.

The warmth of the sun, the softness of the sea air, the drift of haze and sea mist wrap this bit of beach in folds of quietude. It is a spot to come with a good book, with a thick terry towel, and an hour or two to stretch the body and stretch the soul and "extend one's spirit" to meet one's Maker in quiet communion.

Even the birds on the sand, the ground squirrels sunning themselves on the banks of clay, the seals stretched contentedly on the rocks revel in the peace of this place. Here there is respite from the rush and fury of the struggle to survive. Here there is privacy to withdraw from the pressures and rivalry of foraging for food. Here there is relaxation from the rub of life's stresses and strains.

The hours spent in peace here are hours of healing. They are interludes of serenity for the soul, times for making one whole in the world of fragmentation and bruising abuse. The moments slip away softly, their motion as smooth as the murmuring movements of the sea, caressing the conscience, mending the mind, stilling the spirit.

Not only do the southern sun, the pungent sea air, the tingling ocean water turn the body a lovely golden brown, but they also turn the soul into a citadel of contented serenity with the spirit ensconced in quiet rest.

The sea edge is in very tangible truth one of God's great gifts to His earth children—not just exclusively for man, but also for all his brothers of paw, wing, flipper or shell. It is a place to be shared, relished, cherished and preserved. For here one can find wholeness, soundness, health and beauty amid a troubled world.

There are those who rather naively insist that our Father can be found only in the formal and sometimes rather august surroundings of a man-made sanctuary. But my contention is that He is more often met in the majestic amphitheater of His own wondrous creation. He cannot be confined to structures of steel, concrete and glass devised and erected by the efforts of man.

He comes softly to meet the soul open to receive Him upon a stretch of sand, along some leaf-strewn forest trail, across a summer meadow deep in sun-splashed daisies, or on a storm-blasted mountain ridge.

Yes, our God is everywhere present in His universe—even in our bustling canyons of brick and iron that roar with the thunder of our vaunted technology. He is even in our ghettos of grime, and in our luxury condominiums crammed with their ceaseless sound and fury.

The problem is most people will not take either the time or

trouble to find their "place of peace." They cannot be bothered to seek an oasis of serenity in the desert of their drab days. They have never discovered the healing stillness of some quiet spot where they can meet God and know Him in gentle meditation.

Crowded, pressured, driven, desperate, they rush on and on!

It takes time to draw aside from the society of man.

It takes time to enter deliberately into the presence of God.

It takes time to commune with Christ as friend.

For some people such time is simply not available. They feel it is wasted, thrown away, spent for naught. They would prefer to expend it on something much more stirring and exciting—like a football game, a soap opera, or perhaps even the fluctuations of the stock market.

There is a certain discipline of soul, a setting of the will, a determination of spirit required to meet with God's Spirit in a place of peace. It calls for much more than merely feeling like it. It demands a deliberate act of faith that in such a spot I shall meet my God. Such meetings are not encounters arranged by the church, denomination, or assembly of God's people to which I belong. Rather they are a private rendezvous planned purposely, carried out quietly, between me and my Father.

For when I truly am fond of Him, such personal interludes are extremely precious. They are encounters in which Christ communes with me in the very depths of my being. Through His Word and by His Spirit His presence becomes every bit as tangible to my soul and spirit as the touch of the sun on my cheek, the caress of the sea wind on my face, the refreshment of the ocean on my body.

Most of us know very little indeed about opening ourselves to the incoming peace of the presence of The Most High. Rarely do we expose our minds, our emotions, our wills fully to the influence of His Holy Person. We seldom dare to invite the living Lord to search our spirits, cleanse our conscience, enliven our intuition, so bringing us into close communion with Himself—the Christ of eternity, the One who loves us so profoundly. But when we do, we find peace—His peace—for He speaks peace to us.

Peace that passes our human comprehension is not a quality of life which excludes us from the stresses and strains of human society. It is not a sheltered withdrawal from the wrongs that rack our world. Nor is it a cloistered existence in which we are cut off from the calamities and conflicts of our generation.

The place of peace to which God our Father calls us is that intimate inner acquaintance with Himself whereby we come to know so assuredly: "O Father, You are here! All is well!" This is the personal, private encounter with Christ which brings serenity amid the storms of life. It is the pervading influence of His own Spirit, so profound He speaks peace even in the midst of earth's most formidable pressures.

The peace He provides is not such as the world supplies. His peace is of eternal duration. It is as timeless as the tides that shape the sea edge and form my bit of beach. In His peace my soul finds strength, my days find deep delight.

14.

Sound of the Surf

As I sit at my desk writing, long, long before dawn ever tints the eastern horizon with gold, I can clearly hear the voice of the surf on my bit of beach. Some days it is muted and soft like a distant whisper. Other times it is distinct, sharp and emphatic with the clear notes of an ocean orchestra. Occasionally it thunders and booms with the roar of giant breakers bursting like artillery shells against the bluffs.

The sea has many sounds. It speaks in a wide range of accents to those of us who live near it and have come to love its voice. The notes played upon this strip of shore are some of the most sublime music of divine design composed in the cosmos.

The songs of the sea, the murmuring of streams, the running notes of rivers, the thundering of waterfalls, the soft melody of lakes lapping on a shore, the fine music of a fountain flowing over its rocks are all fluid sounds produced by water in motion. In this music of the ages there lies remarkable therapy for the whole of man . . . body, soul and spirit.

Running water, whether in waves, ripples, cascades or

simple oscillation, brings with it a balm to weary bodies—a repose to high-strung souls and a quiet serenity to the human spirit.

Primitive men knew this instinctively. They sought solace and strength and inspiration from the voice of the waters. They spoke in awe and reverence of the singing streams and thundering seas. They came often to the water's edge not just for refreshment but also for the rejuvenation that the water music provided.

For me as a man, a great part of the pure pleasure derived from the sea edge is the loveliness of its sounds. For those not attuned to its music, unaccustomed to its rhythms, there may appear at first a restlessness to its beat upon the beach. But with further acquaintance and increasing intimacy the beach lover comes to know every nuance of the ocean sound, to enjoy the variations of its voice, to respond to the stimulus of its song.

In fact, a large part of the unalloyed fascination of the shore is the symphonic variation of the melodies played upon it. There are days when the sea, under a brittle blue summer sky, barely whispers in soft notes of tiny wavelets caressing the sand . . . like the gentle tones of a violin string section. Other days there is the steady beat of breakers pounding the rocks like drums in the distance. Then there are times when with thundering notes there are the trumpet sounds of great waves rolling in from the deeps—the crash of their breaking on the beach, the clash of cymbals in the hands of the celestial music maker.

In all of this I find enormous stimulation, splendor and joy. The sound of the surf speaks to me at the greatest depths of my being. It is ever there, ever present, ever pervasive. Even though my thoughts and emotions may be preoccupied with other interests and activities, in the background there persists the eternal song of the sea.

Whether my hours on the beach are taken up with reading a book, enjoying a brisk stroll, lost in quiet prayer or simply stretched in the sun thinking long thoughts, the ocean music surrounds and enfolds me with its melodies. It is superior to any stereo sound. It comes to me clearly with the utmost fidelity, untarnished by human technology.

In a word, a large part of the wonder of this music from the deep is that it is there free for the listener. There is no charge for admission. There is no limit to how long one cares to stay and enjoy it. It has neither beginning nor end. Freely it is given, freely it may be received. One can come heavy in heart, downcast in soul, weary in spirit, yet go away renewed. Often after a quiet interlude by the sea my steps turn toward home revitalized and invigorated by the music of the morning. As it sweeps over me in wave upon wave of inspiration, hope and uplift, my spirit and soul are energized by the eternal music of the spheres. My whole person is at peace with the benediction of God, my Father's, blessing.

He chooses to speak to us earthlings in various ways. His thoughts and intentions toward me as His child are clearly articulated in many modes. We speak freely of "hearing His voice" and being attuned to His purposes. The Scriptures are replete with references to the songs of love that come to the bride from the Beloved. There is the sound of the Shepherd communing with His sheep.

In music of as many moods as that produced by the ocean upon the shore, God's gracious Spirit plays upon the shore of my soul. Sometimes He speaks to me in the softest whispers. It may be a gentle suggestion from His Word, the kindly remark of a caring friend, the refrain from a song, the momentary impact of an exquisite sunset or the serenity of a star-studded night.

In that fleeting, sublime instant, my spirit, quietly responsive to Christ's presence, is sensitive to His voice. I sense acutely I have heard from Him. He is here. All is well. The music of His companionship cheers me. The melody of His good will assures me He is near. He has spoken to my spirit.

On other occasions His Spirit, through His Word, comes to

me with great force and profound conviction. He speaks loudly, clearly. As pervasive and powerful as the ocean is upon my bit of beach, so equally is the presence and power of Christ in the life of His intimate companions. There come times in the life of the earnest Christian when all of his experiences are under the influence and touch of the Master. It is God, the very God, who, at work upon his life, produces music not of his making.

The shore does not compose the melodies played out upon its strand. The sea does! The shore does not shape the sounds of the surf. The ocean does! The beach is but the amplifier from which there emerges the score of the Maestro.

So it is with me. If there is to emerge from my brief and fleeting sojourn here any music of eternal worth, it must be of my Master's making. My spirit attuned to His can reverberate with the rhythms of eternity. My soul in resonant response to His voice can reflect the joyous music of my God. Out of the innermost depths of my being, can come melodies arranged and scored in the sanctuary of The Most High.

As eternal as the surge of the sea, so is the ever moving melody of the love of God my Father flowing over me. As soothing as the sound of the surf, so is the quiet assurance that sweeps over my soul that Christ is my constant companion, speaking peace to my spirit. As inspiring and thrilling as the thunder of the breakers on the beach, so is the strong surge of God's Spirit breaking in upon my life. In a hundred places, in a score of ways, He is ever pressing in upon me to inspire with great joy in songs of praise.

Yes, yes! There are grand and splendid sounds on the shore of my sea edge. But there can be music and melodies just as glorious and wondrous played on the strand of my life. It is freely available if I will but give Him the time.

15.

Bluffs and Cliffs

In several of the earlier chapters of this book passing reference was made to the rock bluffs and sandstone cliffs along my bit of beach. In large part they are what contribute to its striking character. They give this part of the coast a strength and seclusion that makes it very special in nature.

Many mornings, even in the worst of winter weather, I am profoundly impressed with the dramatic change in climate as I descend the trail that winds down the cliffs. It is like stepping down into the warmth of a solarium. The sunshine, soft as it may be with the winter sun low on the horizon, is trapped by the cliffs and reflected back upon the beach.

This solar heat combined with the thermal warmth of the ocean itself creates a remarkable micro-climate along the foot of the cliffs. Here temperatures may be as much as twenty degrees warmer than up on the windswept meadows above the beach. The imposing bluffs break the force of breezes blowing from the high mountains to the north. So the shore becomes a secret Shangri-la for men and wildlife who seek its pleasant sanctuary.

Here flocks of sea birds, gulls, pelicans, curlews and sand-pipers come to rest on the sands. Some of them, weary with their long migratory flights up and down the Pacific flyway, pause here to rest their wings and preen their plumage.

Here red-tailed hawks, kestrels and even crows ride the thermals and forage for food along the bluffs. Herons and egrets soar on the warm winds rising along the cliffs, their snow white wings sharp against the blue sky.

At low tide the sea-washed sand, smooth as a piece of ancient pewter, damp with shining sea water, reflects the grandeur of the bluffs as in a mirror. Their golden, tawny faces and rugged gray ramparts appear doubly impressive when viewed from the sea edge. Somehow they look so massive, so stalwart, so eternal, so enduring.

But in reality they are not!

The forces of weathering are ever at work on them.

Their character is one of constant change.

The pounding of the surf, the crash of giant waves, the working of the wind, the rivulets of winter rain, the lashing of seasonal storms off the sea, the variation of temperatures from day to night—all erode, sculpt and shape the character of the cliffs.

Some of these bold bluffs may have withstood ten thousand storms. But then one day a giant fault will appear in the cliff face. In time a thundering avalanche of rock, soil, and debris will crash to the foot of the rampart. Rocks, rubble and scattered stone will lie shattered on the sand.

It takes time and hundreds of tides to wear this material away. The running of the sea currents, the rasping of the sand, the softening of the sea water will do their unceasing work to beautify the beach again. For the cliffs, like the sand, are in eternal flux. They know only endless change. They are at best the passing reflection of an ever-changing seascape.

Yet, in a wondrous way, this is all a part of the eternal

fascination of the sea edge. There is nothing static or sterile about it. Subject to the action of the ocean it is being altered from strength to strength, from glory to glory, from character to character. It is not stale, but stimulating.

Often as I wander quietly along the foot of the seacliffs I am reminded vividly that my own life is just like they are. My own character is just as subject to change. There really is nothing about my person which cannot be altered by the passing of the seasons.

There are, it seems to me in moments of quiet reflection, areas of our lives where we seem to be very similar to sand on the shore. Our minds and emotions are easily moved, played upon, and shaped readily by the current of events and circumstances God arranges around us.

The influence of people, the impact of the beauty of the natural world, the care and affection of family and friends, the attention of our associates, the flow of time and study and knowledge shape our thoughts and mold our emotions rather easily.

But standing in sharp and solid contrast, like the bluffs above the beach, there tower over our lives the strong, formidable bulwarks of our tough wills. The hard rock of our apparently invulnerable volition is like a bastion of basalt against the storms of life.

Of course I can only speak with authenticity about this inner bastion of the will from my own personal perspective. Yet, from what I have observed in the lives of others, it appears to hold equally true for them as well. For ultimately, man's volition, tough and hard as it may appear, is subject to change under the impact of God's presence and the circumstances of change which Christ can arrange in our careers.

It is the man whose spirit has been shaped by the weathering wind of God's Spirit; whose hard heart has been broken by the breaking power of our Father's love; whose tough will has been altered by the touch of the Master's hand, who becomes a beautiful character.

He may be as rough and rugged as the rock ramparts rising at the sea edge on my bit of beach. He may seem as scarred and chiselled by the work of the world as are the cliffs by the attrition of wind and water. He may appear as worn and twisted by the conflicts and storms of life as the bluffs above the beach. But despite it all, there is a striking dignity, a strong serenity, a tender warmth to the fortitude sculpted in his face by a thousand storms.

There will be faults and cracks in the character of the man who has withstood the endless stresses of many changing tides. But under the great, good hand of God, each mark, each line, each change in the contour of his character will but enhance its appeal. It is under the shaping, chiselling forces of life's varied experiences that Christ can sculpt us into magnificent masterpieces if we will but let Him. These are the well-worn tools of His trade for turning out beautiful souls. His Spirit can work wonders on the rough stone of our tough wills, bringing them into lovely conformity to His own will.

It is this sort of person, who, standing tall, despite the worst weather, reflects back something of the warmth and wholesomeness of Christ. As the sandstone cliffs with open face to the southern sun create their own marvelous mini-climate on the coast, so the man open to the impact of the "Sun of Righteousness," reflects something of God's love to a weary world around him.

There is a warmth, an appeal, a quiet serenity in the presence of such a person. Constantly there goes on a change, a transformation, a transition from glory to glory, from character to character as the gracious Spirit of God moves upon a submissive spirit.

In the shaping of such a life others find a place of peace, an oasis of repose. It is in the work, the words, the silent influence of such a person attuned to the will of God that men and women, boys and girls, animals and even plants will thrive and flourish.

The strong people, the sturdy souls, the quietly contented characters whose impact goes on without their realizing it, are ever a benediction to both God and man in the world. Even long after they are gone, changed and transformed into the enduring dimension of eternity, their gracious, glowing endowments will remain to enrich our lives.

It has been my rare privilege to walk softly in company with some such souls. They have done me every bit as much good as the bluffs along my beach. Through their words, by their friendship, in their letters and writing, from their memoirs, God has used their characters to touch and change my own.

These have been the reflectors of His grace and goodness to me. I am rich for having known them. My earnest prayer and ardent hope is that I, in turn, may have been a bulwark of strength and assurance to others who sought solace in my company.

16.

Winter Weather

On the coast of southern California, where I live, pleasant weather prevails most of the year. In fact, our short strip of shoreline, running roughly east and west for about thirty miles, is one of the few areas in North America blessed with a true Mediterranean climate. Here the sun shines, at least for several hours, most days of the year. And, very rarely does this bit of beach remain wrapped in rain and dampness more than a day or two at a time.

Still, occasional winter storms surge out of the Pacific. Freighted with dark clouds bearing warm subtropical moisture they move in over the coastal mountains, powered by oceanic pressure systems. The rain pours down in heavy deluges that send sheets of water streaming across the countryside.

Very quickly the excess flood waters gather in every stream, creek and river bed. Many of these are dry, sundrenched trenches most of the year. But now they are suddenly filled with cascading, rumbling flows of silt-laden water. They pick up soil, sand, debris and driftwood that is carried down to the ocean in flooding torrents.

Suddenly the sea is stained brown and red with the river silt. The ocean, under leaden gray skies, surges onto the shore, driven by the wind, in dark waves laden with mud and debris from the land. Along the line of high tide a windrow of broken wood, logs, planks and tangled branches litters the shore.

Rivulets of stained water cascade off the cliffs. They carve sharp, ragged wounds in the face of the bluffs. The rain streams down from the black sky in sheets. The low dark clouds rumble with thunder. The sea roars!

The sound of the surf storming against the shoreline can be heard like a distant roll of drums in the distance. Even under the pall of the heavy overcast, the ocean still bursts into white breakers that appear almost ghostlike and ominous in the stormy darkness. Sometimes the cross currents running in the sea are so strong the waves crash across each other moving in different directions at the same time.

The thunderous action of the combers clawing at the beach will strip away the sand, laying bare the shore bed of rock and rubble. The howling of the wind; the churning of the sea; the tangle of driftwood and shattered seaweed tossed up by the tides; the bleak, gaunt barrenness of the coast during such a storm leave the impression of utter desolation.

Those not familiar with my bit of sea edge are often dismayed by the spectacle of damage during a heavy "blow." Yet, always I am reassured that the beach will not long remain battered and bruised. Its beauty will be restored. The ocean will bring back the sand. The silt and mud and debris will be borne away into the ocean's canyon deeps. The sun will break through the clouds again. And in the place of winter's turmoil, there will be repose and rest once more.

Promise of this often comes with a beautiful rainbow. I recall vividly one evening going down to walk on the storm-battered beach. It had been a most difficult day, dark not only because of the howling storm, but also dreary because of painful reverses in other areas of life. It seemed I had never seen the beach in such disarray, stripped of its lovely sand, strewn with storm wreckage. It exactly matched the melancholy mood of my own inner spirit, grieved and torn with trouble.

I stumbled over the wet stones, hunching my back against the gale; grimly I pulled the big wool sweater tight around my chest; I uttered a silent prayer of relief and respite. "O Father, reassure me You are here!"

In a matter of moments an exquisite, brilliant, glowing rainbow began to arch over the beach. One end was anchored on the dark brooding bluffs. The other stood strongly amid the surging black and white breakers in the sea. Arched over the agony of a storm-stripped beach with its broken piles of shattered driftwood and scattered flotsam shone the wondrous colors of the most beautiful rainbow I had ever seen.

Their intensity was so pronounced they pulsed with glowing light, caught from the low rays of the sun breaking through the dark overcast of the clouds. Suddenly in a blaze of golden glory the whole coast and ocean edge was awash in a glow of burnished light. I was too moved in spirit to keep walking. Awestruck I stood alone, still and beyond words on the storm-ravaged shore.

Wave upon wave of enormous emotion swept through my soul. Impulse upon impulse of powerful reassurance inundated my spirit. In the splendor of the rainbow I sensed again the eternal, enduring goodness of my God. In the blaze of light from the setting sun I saw acutely the changeless character of Christ. Like Noah of old, after the dreadful ordeal of the flood, I sensed again the presence and promise of the almighty Spirit of the Eternal God: *"I am here. All is well. Fear not."*

Gently, softly, the rainbow began to fade. Ever so slowly that evening the last faint colors drained from the scene. The afterglow of the setting sun seemed to linger longer than usual. Everywhere there was peace.

In utter rest and with total composure I again began to stroll along the shore a short distance. Then in quiet repose I turned my steps toward home, refreshed in spirit, at peace in my mind.

Tomorrow the sun would warm these shores again. Tomorrow the ocean current would bring back the sand. Tomorrow the curling waves would cleanse away the filth, covering the ravages of the storm. Tomorrow this sea edge would sparkle with fresh brilliance.

Life for God's child is like that. Just because we belong to Him, does not exempt us from the dark storms and heavy weather of life. We must, and can expect, that in the short sojourn of our brief years here there will be some gales of adversity, some "blows" off the open seas of our days.

But the stirring truth remains that for those of us who know and love Him, our Father is always there with us. As the ancient prophet Nahum declared so boldly: "The Lord hath His way in the whirlwind and in the storm, and the clouds are the dust of His feet" (1:3).

He is ever active in our affairs. He is ever reliable in arranging the circumstances of our lives behind the scenes. He is ever near us moving on our behalf to bring about changes that are intended for our good. In the darkest hours we find Him closest.

The storms of life come and go. The winter weather is but for a short season. The dark squalls and gusting winds are passing phenomena. When they are gone, the rainbow of God's blessing and reassurance remind us of His presence. The unique peace which He alone can provide for His people pervades our spirits. And the rest He promises us endures as our legacy. All of us have winter weather. We face those formidable interludes in life when everything looks dark and depressing. We all have times when our days are strewn with the apparent wreckage of wrong choices and derelict decisions. The best of men and women know what it is to be stripped down to the bedrock of sheer survival.

Yet amid all such storms what a consolation to know our Father has His strong hand upon us for our own good. What an assurance to recognize that Christ can be counted on to control the final outcome of our apparent calamities. What a strength to see His gracious Spirit bring great glory and beauty out of what to us may have seemed only disastrous!

Tomorrow is always His. It belongs to Him.

He can make it mine as well!

17.

Winter Rains and Beach Flowers

The Southern California coast is world renowned for its glorious sunshine. Its beautiful beaches are a mecca for millions who love the sea and enjoy the surf. Near the metropolitan centers, homes and harbor structures crowd the shoreline. Concrete, steel, glass and brick dominate the landscape. The shore remains not much more than a strip of sand betwixt sea and land.

But where I live, the coast is still very much as it was when the first Spanish explorers set foot upon its shores. There are meadows of native grass and wild flowers that flourish along the beach. Here and there clusters of California sycamores and oaks march down the canyons to the sea, while along the cliffs a scattering of native plants and shrubs grace the bluffs casting a network of fragile growth over the ever-eroding land formations.

I have always been astonished at just how hardy and persistent these coastal wild flowers are. For though the climate may seem soft and gentle, in reality, where they are rooted on the abrupt beach bluffs, it is tough and stern. There are some seasons when, apart from fog and ocean mist, they never receive a drop of rain for months on end. The surface of the soil is heated to high temperatures and the earth bakes hard as a brick road.

In fact, one type of soil, common to this area, is a rich black clay known throughout the Southwest as "adobe." In the long summer droughts it becomes as tough as concrete and as durable as rock. Yet under the touch of winter rain it becomes soft, plastic, soaked with a massive amount of moisture like a great sponge.

It is the warm sea showers of our winter season that bring about such a spectacular transformation of the coastal terrain. The brown, golden hills of summer that stretch down to the sea like a blanket of bronze become an emerald green. This mantle of grass pulses with a green glory which no words can adequately describe. It is of such shining intensity and serene iridescence that after a warm winter rain it seems more like a dream than reality.

Often as I move along the shore it appears so utterly beautiful, so completely perfect, so exquisitely lovely that it is akin to walking across a painted stage setting. On one side the blue Pacific stretches away to the horizon. Along its fringe of beach, the rolling surf lays a lacework of immaculate white across the golden sand. On the other side, the shoreline itself undulates above the brown, buckskin cliffs in a gorgeous carpet of green grass and blowing wild flowers.

The wild flowers come in many hues and shades. There are brilliant beach peas of flaming pink. I have gathered some of their seed and planted them in my own garden. What a show they made, spreading out into huge clumps of bursting blooms. The tough and hardy ice plants, turgid with the winter rain, burst into colors as varied as a rainbow. There are yellows, reds, purples and pinks, some of them so prolific they appear as rugs of flowers flung at random over the cliffs and rocks.

Sea Birds

Sea birds are one of the most fascinating, as well as beautiful, creatures of our coastline. Not only are they an integral part of the seascape all year, but the sound of their cries rings over the beach in wild melodies that match the music of the surf.

It so happens that because of the great diversity of terrain along this ocean edge, it provides a wide variety of habitat suited to many species of birds. Both land and sea birds intermingle along the shore. For here the mountains meet the sea. Foothills run their sun-warmed feet into the surf. Creeks, streams and seasonal water courses create lagoons and salt water marshes where birds abound. Open meadows, deep in wild grass and brush, with a scattering of native trees, run along the shoreline. High cliffs and lofty bluffs provide updrafts upon which raptors love to soar in search of rodents and insects.

It is almost impossible to stroll along my bit of beach without encountering a score of feathered friends. Some, like the gulls, cormorants, terns and pelicans, skim softly just above the waves. They wheel and circle and cry in the wind.

133

Sea Birds

Some days when wild weather is in the offing they will soar high into the sky, mere specks in the wind, cutting silent circles against the gathering clouds.

If shoals of herring or anchovies are running in the current, flocks of sea birds follow them in wild excitement. Plunging, diving, circling and splashing into the sea with wild abandon, the birds feed on the silver hordes with incredible frenzy. In great flocks they come winging in from the channel islands to feast on the ocean bounty. Then, at last, replete with fresh fish they settle softly on the shore.

There are mornings when I have counted well over a thousand gulls in a single flock resting on the wet sand where the tide recedes. Their gorgeous white and gray plumage is mirrored in the reflecting surface of the shore. Their vast number of multicolored shapes lie like a beautiful quilt of gray and white flung at random across the beach.

Intermingled among the gulls are somber pelicans standing silently in stately dignity. Here and there are a few pairs of curlews, yellowlegs or whimbrels preening themselves in the morning sunshine. Everywhere there is an aura of peace, serenity and well-being amongst the birds.

As I approach, they lift off gently into the breeze, circle softly around me to alight again on the sand behind my back. In front of me there are often energetic, erratic little flocks of sanderlings and sandpipers. With exciting energy and flying feet they feed tirelessly between the waves that wash across the shore.

If startled or alarmed, the shining birds flash away from the surf, skim over the waves, banking and wheeling with breath-taking precision. The movement of their tiny forms in perfect formation reflects the light in brilliant colors from shining silver to pure white or beaten pewter. To watch them fly in such marvelous, intricate patterns without confusion or collision is to be thrilled and stimulated with pure pleasure.

The same sensation comes to me as I follow the fairylike

flight of the delicate terns that skim above the sea. Their lightness, their brightness, their beautiful swift wingbeats above the water rivet my attention with breathless exhilaration. It is almost as if they are angels of light hovering over the shore.

No two species of birds have precisely the same life pattern. Their movements on the sand, their search for sustenance from the sea, their flight formation, their form and rate of wingbeat, their cries in the ocean wind are all different and engaging. Each has found its own niche here in the complex pattern of ocean life. Each brings to the beach its own unique beauty and inspiration. Each enlivens and enriches my days along the shore.

Often as I watch the birds I am deeply impressed with the concept that they are as much an integral part of the shore as sand or sea or shell or stone. It may be at times they are only transients, visitors, moving up and down the Pacific flyway from the Arctic to South America. Still they are a part of the pulsing ebb and flow of the sea life that surrounds me. They are in constant motion as much as the surge of the surf or the wind over the water.

They are in truth one of the beautiful bonuses so richly bequeathed upon all of us who love the shore and spend a part of our lives there.

It is exactly the same in our life with the Lord. Often, so often, I am profoundly impressed by the beauty of the bountiful bonuses He brings to my days. I can never be sure what sudden shining surprises He will inject into my experience.

Like the birds on the beach, there are those times when their numbers are so great I am overwhelmed with the impact of their presence. I cannot help but pause and stand in awe, overwhelmed by the myriads of wings soaring against the sky or smoothly burnished bodies resting quietly on the sand. There are birds on every side—birds above, birds around me, birds before my feet.

So it is with life. There are days when the marvelous blessings of my Father come winging in upon me in such abundance I can scarcely comprehend the outpouring of His generosity. There are days when in awe and wonder I can only lift my heart in praise, my spirit in adoration, for all the bounties He bestows upon the beach of my life.

The benefits come from far and near. Some are letters, phone calls, messages from friends in the family of God that stir my spirit, quicken my pulse, inspire my outlook. Others are close at hand—the loveliness of the land, green hills after the rain, warm earth after the storm, sunshine through the clouds, the beauty of the flowers, the voice of a friend, the smile of a stranger, the companionship of a dear one.

Like the birds along the beach each is designed and ordered of God to enrich my days and enliven my world. They are gifts from the sea. They come at no cost. They charge no fee. They are there, free, for the one who will pause to receive their uplift and inspiration.

Other days on the beach are not as replete and full with birds. Still there are always some there. It may take a little time to find a solitary curlew or a single tern. But they are to be found. And in the spread of a mottled pair of wings with gorgeous tan feathers or in a single flash of white wings over the waves there lies enormous inspiration.

The best of blessings do not always come in crowds.

There are those still, quiet moments when alone in gentle communion with Christ I sense and see the momentary glory of His person. The intense nearness of His Spirit as soft, yet sublime, as any tern on wing, moves my spirit. And again I know, "O Father, You are here! I have been enriched by Your beautiful bonuses."

As with the lone and sometimes solitary sea birds on the beach, there are times when we must search and seek for the bonus blessings of our God.

Yesterday I went to walk alone on the shore. In mid-winter it appeared desolate, empty and forlorn. Its mood exactly matched the melancholy of my own emotions. I had been seriously ill for several weeks. Strength was slow to return. Responsibilities and work were falling far behind, overwhelming me with their pressures.

As I strolled alone along the sand, suddenly my attention was arrested by a magnificent snow-white heron soaring on the thermals above the beach. Herons seldom do this. Usually their flight is slow, ponderous and heavy. Yet this beautiful bird sailed in utter serenity, scarcely moving a wing, gliding in rhythmic circles against the brilliant blue sky. Finally it soared down to settle sedately on the crown of a wind-tossed Monterey cypress clinging to the cliffs.

At once my spirit was inspired. My emotions were moved. My whole being was galvanized by the splendor and glory of this sight.

Out of the silence, out of the stillness, out of the serenity of that moment my Father spoke to me in accents only His: "My son, you are not forgotten. I am here to help, to heal, to lift you above the burdens of life!"

I needed no more. I had seen a vision of beauty. My life had been enriched by the bounty of my Father's bonus.

At dawn today, with renewed strength I got up and began to write this chapter. It was the first solid, fresh work done in long weeks of weakness.

Yes, our Father is ever faithful. But there are days when we must seek and search to find the presence of His person. Then, when we do, what a delight!

We are set free, free, free, as any bird on wing against the blue.

19.

Broken Rocks and Smooth Stones

One of my favorite beach hikes takes me roughly two miles along the shoreline. The trail winds over a variety of coastal terrain. There is a steep path that first leads down an eroded coulee where a small seep of water trickles down the cliffs to the sea. Here a beautiful warm sand beach arches against the clay cliffs in a soft, half-moon bay.

Beyond the bay a bold headland of sandstone formation juts out into the sea. It is rugged, with wind-chiseled caves underlying the shelves of stone. Native ice plants and wild shrubs cascade over its rough features. Often, under the weathering of Pacific storms, giant slabs of the sandstone formation crash down on the boulders below.

Here bit by bit the huge rocks are rolled and tumbled in the high surf until their surfaces are smooth as satin. It is not easy to hike across these rock piles. Their character is never constant. Every "big blow" and every extreme high tide shifts the stones, rearranging their positions in the pile.

Once past this point, the sea edge trail runs out onto wide shelves of gray rock that lie open to the sea. In spots, these slabs of smooth bed rock appear as eternal as the sea itself. But they are not. The relentless battering of the surf, the sledgehammer impact of a thousand storms, the hydraulic compression of mountainous waves crack the rock and shatter the stone.

Bit by bit, week by week, year after year the fortresslike formations are slowly reduced to rubble. One spot in particular, swept clean by the sea, is a favorite spot of mine to spread a towel and stretch out in the sun after a brisk swim. Here I lie alone to relax and read. Yet I am ever aware that the rock around me is constantly changing.

Hairline cracks appear in its surface. With the rush and thrust of incoming tides the fissures open wider under the weight and pressure of the sea. Fragments of rock are broken from the bedrock. Then in time these boulders are shattered and tumbled in the ocean until reduced to small smooth stones.

Passing these outcrops of rock and smooth shelves of stone, the beach trail leads on to yet another gorgeous stretch of sand. Scattered here and there along its upper edge are windrows of small stones and exquisite, multicolored pebbles shaped by the sea. Many of these little stones are of delicate hue and attractive shape. Some are so beautiful in texture and color that they make lovely jewelry.

I have picked up translucent agates and snow-white stones of such perfection that they made lovely pendants my wife delighted to wear.

A short distance down this great sweeping beach that extends for several miles along the coast stands a group of giant conglomerate boulders. They are as huge as a cluster of haystacks. They stand like giant sentinels on the sand, their rugged character chiseled and sculpted by the surf that beats against them.

They, too, are gradually being broken by the sea. They, too, are slowly being shattered into smaller pieces. They, too, one day, will be reduced to small smooth stones that lie wet and lustrous, shining upon the sand.

Then someone will pick up a piece and bear it home as a special treasure gathered between the tides.

These small smooth stones are not something to be hoarded and gathered only for one's self. They are bits of beauty to be displayed upon a window ledge, to be shared with friends, to be passed on with happiness to children who come to visit in our home.

In His own special way God has often spoken to me distinctly through the stones on my bit of beach. In their beauty and attractiveness I have been made to see that some of the choicest treasures in life come to us through a long history of hardship.

Small shining stones are not shaped in a day. They are not formed in a single storm. They do not emerge to lie shining in the sun from the turbulence of one night's tide.

They are the end product of a long and painful process that has gone on for countless years and scores of stormy seasons. Small smooth stones once stood as sturdy rock ridges or rugged bedrock. Broken and battered by countless thundering seas, they have been shaped to ultimate perfection in the rolling mills of tide and surf. Their smooth surface emerges from the rugged rasping of sand, the grinding of gravel in the rock tumbler of the tides.

Our lives, too, are like that. It takes the hard and sometimes shattering events of life to break our hard hearts. It takes calamities and losses to crack and fracture our bold, brave facade. It takes the surge of sorrows, the grinding of grief to shatter our proud spirits, our tough, hard wills.

Most of us don't want to be broken in the storms of life. We much prefer to protect our personalities from the stresses and strains of our days. We would rather, much rather, be tough and rugged and self-assured than contrite before Christ, repentant in soul before His Spirit.

No, as the rocks resist the action of the sea that surrounds them, so we resist the movement of our God who enfolds us in His encircling care. We see the impact of His presence upon us as something shattering, painful and at times very unpleasant.

Many of us would like to avoid the mills of God. We are tempted to ask Him to deliver us from the upsetting, tumbling tides of time that knock off our rough corners and shape us to His design. We plead for release from the discipline of difficulties, the rub of routine responsibilities, the polish that comes from long perseverance.

We are a restless generation. We of the West want and insist on instant results. We demand a quick-fix. We look for shortcuts and immediate results. We are quite sure we can be a rough slab of stone today and a polished gemstone tomorrow.

But God's ways and our ways are not the same. His patience is persistent. His work is meticulous. His years know no end. His perception of time is that one day is as a thousand years and a thousand years as but a single day.

The shattering of rock, the smoothing of stone, the polishing of a jewel in the sea requires eons of time. Can I then expect the breaking of my hard heart, the smoothing of my spirit, the shaping of my character as it is conformed to His own to be any less time-consuming?

If it takes fifty years to fashion a gemstone on the shore, can it not be understood that it will take a lifetime for my character to be made into the likeness of Christ?

The tides of time—the endless surf of changing circumstances, the tumbling of unexpected events, the eternal pressure of His presence, the washing of His Word that sweeps over my soul, the stimulation and surge of His Spirit, the polish of His mercy and kindness and love—will leave me

lying contented, smooth, and shining in the glory of His Sun.
This all takes time.
This all takes care.
This all occurs in the ocean of His providence
for me as His person.
And because of it all, one day He will see fit to pick me up
off the sands of time. He will bear me away home with Him as
a special treasure. For I shall be one who has been fashioned
under His watchful eye to be one of His small, smooth stones,
a jewel of great worth in His estimation.
What good cheer this is for the child of God!

20.

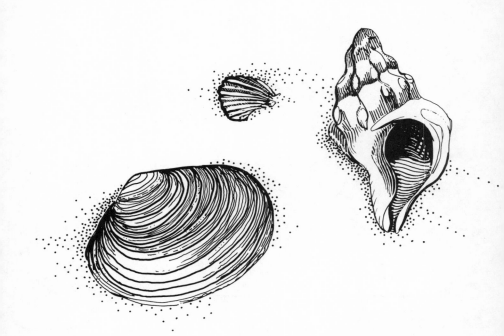

Shells along the Shore

Seashells have played a rather unusual role in our home. In a strong yet gentle way they are a constant reminder to us of the sea we love so much. They speak of the summer sands, of low tides, of roaring surfs, of quiet interludes in company with the ocean edge.

The moment one enters our front door, it is to see a gorgeous twisted driftwood root surrounded by shells. There are shells of all sorts adorning the window ledges. Shells of spectacular shape and color are on display amongst our bookshelves. A small basket of minute shells stands on a beautiful burl table. Its contents are reserved for children who visit us and wish to bear home a choice gift from the sea in their hot little hands.

It is the sharing of shells which has come to mean so much to us. My wife has fashioned exquisite pendants from choice shells which she gives to her friends on special occasions. Often when I return from a stroll along the shore I will bear in my well-worn pockets a lovely specimen or two for her. At the sight of them her warm brown eyes glow with pleasure and a winsome smile steals across her features. *"Just for me!"* she murmurs happily.

All of this may sound rather ordinary to the reader, and it would be if we lived where seashells are abundant. But on my bit of beach they are not. Here at our edge of the sea the crash and roll of the surf is so constant, the grinding and tumbling of the waves so tremendous, that few shells survive intact. Most are shattered.

For me "shell hunting" means just that. There are often days when not a single unbroken specimen can be found anywhere on the sand. Of those which remain undamaged only the thickest, heaviest and toughest seem able to endure the grinding of the ocean mills.

Scattered here and there in sheltering crevices amongst the rocks one can sometimes come across a lovely shell. Half buried in the gravel, sheltered a bit by the surrounding stones, some of the more frail and delicate specimens do survive the breaking of the surf that roars around them.

Perhaps it is because of their comparative scarcity on our coast that the shells cast up on our shore seem of special worth. It is because they are rather rare that they seem to possess a special value out of all proportion to their appearance. For many of them lack the ornate shapes or exotic colors of shells gathered in warmer waters.

Still, for me, finding fine shells remains a happy fascination that has never diminished across the years. Somehow they are one of the beautiful bonuses that come to us from the bounty of the sea. They are gifts bestowed freely for the taking.

As I pick up a shell, wash the clinging sand from its surface, and feel its form between my fingers it elicits awe and admiration from within. The special shape, the delicate designs in its surface, the smooth flow of its convolutions, the exquisite hues of its colors, the sheer loveliness of its form command my attention and draw from my spirit genuine gratitude.

All of this happens the moment I pause in mid-step to stoop down and pick up the treasure from between the tides.

It takes time to do this.

It takes some thought as well.

It takes attention to what the sea is offering.

All of life is like that. Everywhere, scattered here and there along the shore of our lives the tides of time cast up their quota of beautiful bonuses. They may not all be obvious. Some will be less than spectacular. Yet scattered along the strand of our ordinary days it is possible to find precious gifts from God.

There is an old hymn that used to be sung in our sanctuaries much more than it is today. Entitled "Take Time to Be Holy," its theme is that a person who would be whole and wholesome in life has to take the time to be alone with the Lord. There have to be intimate interludes with Christ in which He can convey His life and character to us.

It takes time to look for the special little gifts His gracious Spirit sees fit to bestow upon us in the common round of our daily lives. Like shells upon the sand, they may not always be obvious. They may not be so large we just stumble over them. It may take time and effort and thought to find them. But it can become a habit for us to be constantly on the lookout for bits of divine loveliness and natural beauty all about. There is such a thing as God's child learning to look for the exquisite touch of his Father's hand and heart in the world around him.

It was a veteran missionary working amid the awful poverty, squalor and degradation of India's poor who taught his children early, "Learn to look. Observe quietly. Think long thoughts. Find what is beautiful. Give humble thanks. Recall it to mind often. Refresh your soul in the gentle stream of our Father's bounty!"

To do this is to live with an attitude of gratitude. It is to discover fragments of loveliness in the most ordinary events of life. It is to search and seek and seize every evidence of bonuses bestowed by the gentle hands of our loving Father.

We of the affluent twentieth century have had our sensibilities seared, our appreciation jaded, by the easy overabundance of our days. Few, few amongst us know anything of the humble art of a lowly heart that can find inspiration in the soaring flight of a gull or the exquisite shape of a shell or the song of the surf.

We of the West have, by our crude and crass culture, become so conditioned to look for the sensational and spectacular in our experiences that we miss seeing the stars while looking at our spacecraft. We know so little of the sublime, because we are so attuned to the clash and crash of our civilization. We prefer crowds and mass displays to the enrichment of soul or uplift of spirit that can come to the person prepared to spend a few moments alone in company with Christ.

The Lord is not confined to the pages of Holy Writ.

He is not to be found only in our solemn sanctuaries.

He is not restricted to liturgy or creed.

He is everywhere at work in our weary old world.

He is to be met in a thousand disguises.

His touch is to be found at every turn of the trail.

The point is I must be attuned in spirit, receptive in soul, alert in attitude, to detect the impact of His presence upon my path.

The bonuses of my Father are everywhere about me, scattered at random, freely, like shells upon the shore. But it demands time, thought, attention and perseverance to discover their sheltered spot, their hidden secret places.

Life can be profoundly rich without being pretentious. It can be filled with overflowing vigor if we but pause to relish the fragrance of the breezes that blow across our strand. It can provide an abundance of joy and humor and good will if we seize the seashells scattered along the sands of our times to bear them home to be shared with others. It can be wholesome, hearty, yes, even holy, when we take the time to spend quiet interludes in company with our Father.

Human spirituality does not consist only of creeds, churches, biblical knowledge or good deeds. It is made up as well from the humble art of learning to see and find the impress of my Father's hand in all the land. It is woven into the warp and woof of our little lives by sweet associations in the company of Christ, who cares about sparrows, lillies, and shells from the sea. Human spirituality comes to us afresh every day by His gracious Spirit who touches us with the impress of wind and surf and sea and sky and a thousand glorious sunsets over the shining shore of our days! All for free! All for the taking!

If we will but pause in mid-stride to pick up the treasures of our God from between the tides of time we can become richer in spirit than we ever dreamed.

21.

Sunrise and Sunset

For ocean lovers, sunrise and sunset are perhaps the most poignant interludes of the entire day. These hushed hours bring to the beach a unique aura of splendor and stillness that speak to the innermost spirit of man. They are moments in which often all sense of time is temporarily set aside, to be replaced by awe, wonder and quiet reflection that extends into eternity.

This is especially true of sunrise over the sea. For in this hour of early dawn the shore lies stripped of all human life. The clash and clamor of all human intrusion is stilled. The feverish activity of modern man is absent.

Peace pervades the realm of sea, sky and shore.

Slowly the eastern sky turns from gray to gold, to burning red. The low light casts the coast into sharp silhouettes. Headlands, hills, trees, rocks and birds along the beach stand sharp against the light, cast in brittle black.

The long slender fingers of early dawn reach out from the central palm of the rising sun to stretch themselves across sea and sand. The whole seascape is caught up and wrapped in a golden glow.

If there are random clouds above the horizon they will burn bright with changing colors of crimson, purple and yellow.

A peculiar hush lies heavy over the shore. The sand is swept clean by the overnight tides. And all the world lies fresh, burnished, new as if for the first time it came clean and fresh from the Creator's hand. And in fact it has!

For in truth no two dawns are ever identical.

Nor are the advents of any two days the same.

Each bears a beauty uniquely its own. Each comes with freshness for a new beginning. Each carries the capacity for great adventure, stirring events.

Likewise it is in my humble, quiet walk with God. The imprint made upon the sands of time this dawn are unlike those ever made before.

There stretches before me a strand of eternity upon which may be etched designs of divine inspiration.

It is as clean, clear and uncluttered as any stretch of beach unmarked by the tread of man.

No one has passed this way before.

No one has lived in this moment in this special spot before this time.

No one has left any mark upon this hour.

The dawn announces a new day. It ushers in an untrammeled way. It waits to hear what God will say.

So I am handed a fresh scroll of unfolding time.

What will be inscribed upon it? What designs shall I draw upon the parchment of its hour? What mark or message will be left here of eternal worth and lasting merit?

Every dawn breaks anew upon my soul with the promise that today can be cherished. It is a special treasure of time entrusted to me for the Master's use. It is not bestowed to be

158

squandered in languid living, rather it is received to be emblazoned with impulses and actions of His design.

He is the author and originator of those lasting impressions of divine love, which through my humble hands and lowly heart can decorate this day. Under the gentle stimulus of His winsome Spirit, the spotless scroll of this strand of time can be embroidered with blessings as beautiful as the lacework of white foam on the beach at break of day.

It may be but a fleeting smile, a gracious gesture, a tender thought, yet it leaves an imprint for all of eternity. For in every action there lies a shaping power that changes character for all of time. So in the dawn of each new day comes the chance to be conformed ever more closely to the character of Christ.

It is in the sum total of ten thousand new days—in the accumulated impact of uncounted new sunrises, in the exquisite beauty of unnumbered dawns—that my life can be changed from glory to glory, from character to character, by the pristine splendor of the Spirit of the living Lord who surrounds me with His effulgence.

For just as my soul is stirred and stimulated by the rising of the sun, so, too, my spirit is inspired and quickened by the splendor of the Son of God, whom the psalmist calls the Sun of Glory.

He rises with great healing in His majesty. He rises amongst us bringing new hope for every day. He rises to shed over us mercies and bounties of blessings that are new every morning.

In the acute awareness of all this, life becomes much more than a mere march of time across the calendar. In company with Christ each dawn comes as the beginning of a new chapter in the pageantry of my days.

What is inscribed upon that chapter depends upon the intense sensitivity of my spirit to His. It comes from the willingness of my will to comply with my Father's wishes. It can be beautiful if He is allowed to be the author of my work.

Sunrise and Sunset

Gradually as the sun moves in grandeur across the sky, the hours of the day are flooded with light, warmed with pleasure. Then slowly as evening descends the burning orb of fire settles softly into the sea, as though settling down gently for the night.

The brilliant banners of tattered clouds, tinged with intense red, rose and pulsing scarlet hues, remind us that the day is done. What has been done has been done!

There can be no replay of this day, except in fleeting memory. There can be no rewriting of the script etched upon these hours. With the indelible ink of eternity there has been inscribed upon the page of this eternal sheet of time either something of value, or only what is vain.

Sunset is an hour for quiet reflection. It is the particle of time poised briefly for a brief review of what was done this day. The afterglow closes the chapter, putting a period to the writing of my journal.

Eventide is the time for taking stock of how the day was spent. It calls briefly for a serious evaluation of the manner of my conduct. It speaks softly of work well done, of progress made, of the touch of God's hand upon my life.

It must be hard indeed for skeptics, atheists and agnostics to view sunrises and sunsets. The splendor of their glory, the beauty of their colors, the intensity of their inspiration that comes from our Father's loving heart, are to the unbeliever nothing more than mere chemical and physical responses to external stimuli. No wonder their world is so bleak, their despair so deep, their future so forlorn.

But for God's child sunrise and sunset are very special. They are intense interludes of quiet communion with the living Christ. They are moments of majesty in which our Father displays His love and might. They are scenes of spiritual exaltation in which His glorious Spirit lifts us to wondrous heights of pure joy in His presence.

Again and again across the passing seasons of my years,